man's
information
system

man's information system

A Primer for Media Specialists and Educational Technologists

Robert M. W. Travers

Western Michigan University

CHANDLER PUBLISHING COMPANY

An Intext Publisher • Scranton, Pennsylvania 18515

Contents

Figures

Preface

This book is an outgrowth of a project sponsored many years ago by the United States Office of Education in which an attempt was made to bring together some of the knowledge available about perception, learning, information theory, and neurophysiology, that might have implications for the design of audiovisual materials. The reports coming out of the project were highly technical and reached mainly those interested in research on problems of media. Nevertheless, demand for the project reports came from many countries scattered over the world, a fact which demonstrated the widespread interest in the disciplines that may provide a basis for the design of auditory and visual educational materials. Five years has now elapsed since the original reports of the project were made available, and during these years there have been considerable additions to the knowledge available, and also a growing body of students interested in specializing in media and educational technology. These students need to be exposed to some of the basic knowledge that underlies the area of technology in which they plan to carve out a career. With this group in mind, the present book was planned.

The book is designed as a second textbook for those enrolled in courses in the audiovisual, media, or educational-technology areas. It is not designed as a primary textbook in any of these areas, but could well form a companion volume to the more typical books used. The content is believed to make it particularly appropriate as a text to accompany any of the commonly used texts in the audiovisual area.

Since most of the textbooks in first courses in educational psychology fail to expose the student to any of the modern information-processing models of learning, this book might also be used in conjunction with these textbooks in basic courses in teacher-education programs.

I am grateful to Mary Jane Fenton for her work on the illustrations and to Kathy Weaver for long hours in preparing the final draft of the manuscript.

Robert M. W. Travers

Western Michigan University
July 1969

man's information system

Chapter 1

Man's Information-Reception Systems

Although our advanced technology has produced an impressive proliferation of devices and techniques for providing children with experiences of educational value, the design of these experiences has been undertaken without much influence from the impressive body of emerging knowledge in the areas of perception and learning. Indeed, an examination of any of the widely used textbooks in the audiovisual field shows an extraordinary absence of chapters on such topics as the perceptual systems, perception as information processing, and perceptual coding. Although such texts provide criteria for evaluating products in the "new media," these criteria also reflect little influence of relevant knowledge available in the behavioral sciences. The time is long overdue for such knowledge to have impact.

The Values of Research

New scientific understanding, with implications for practice, generally has to compete with tradition. Although research may show that particular materials or pieces of equipment sold to schools are not as effectively designed as they should be or that they represent obsolete means of instruction, what is established in the marketplace tends to persist, particularly when a substantial profit is involved. Economic factors are much more likely to govern the sales of equipment and materials to schools than are questions of their effectiveness in terms of established principles of perception and learning.

A volume such as this, which attempts to summarize knowledge relevant to the design of audiovisual materials, does not provide the simple and concise recipes that the practitioner typically demands. Indeed, research does not provide a simple set of rules that the practitioner can easily follow. So that the audiovisual practitioner may know what research can or cannot provide for him before he embarks on the study of this book, a few comments on this matter are in order. A reader who works through the material presented here and who looks for hot practical tips on how to develop or present audiovisual materials will be looking for what cannot be here and may end up by learning nothing. The problem of such a reader is that he has been looking for the wrong thing and expects to receive the kind of help that research can rarely give. What, then, does research do for the practitioner?

One of the most immediate effects of research is *to provide a vocabulary* so that the problems of practical areas can be discussed with greater precision than was formerly possible. For example, as a result of research, one no longer has to talk in rather vague terms about how "difficult" or how "easy" a particular narrative accompanying a film appears to be. Today it is possible to make an analysis of narratives in quite specific terms. One can specify the difficulty level of the vocabulary involved both in terms of word counts and in terms of direct measures of the comprehensibility of words. One can obtain measures of the complexity level of the sentence structure. One can also measure the intelligibility of a sample of the words spoken in the particular narration. This improved precision, in turn, enables one to begin to pinpoint the reasons why a particular narrative is difficult for, say, sixth-graders. Again, the language of classical information theory enables one to discuss the characteristics of some instructional materials and to point to features that have a high *information* content and those that are highly *redundant* in the information they provide.

The audiovisual area has been particularly lacking in a technical language that permits the discussion of information communication in even moderately precise terms. At least, the terms typically found in text books on the subject are no more precise than those found in common language. The hope is that the reader will leave this book equipped with a vocabulary that will permit him to make more precise statements about phenomena in his professional field than he would otherwise be able to make.

Research does more than improve the precision of the language of the practitioner. It also permits him *to think more intelligently* about the problems he encounters. John Dewey, long ago (1929), in an illuminating discussion of the relationship of basic disciplines to education, pointed out that although the teacher has long looked to research for simple rules to guide his teaching, research does not provide these, but may permit him to think more intelligently about his problems and to plan more intelligent courses of action. Dewey used examples from history of this impact of research on practice. He pointed out that although Isaac Newton developed a set of principles that had application to the understanding of the stresses operating in structures, his work did not have any immediate impact on bridge design. Indeed, bridges built after Newton looked very much like bridges built before Newton, but bridge builders after Newton were able to approach their problems in subtle new ways that had been opened up for them. They were able, for example, to calculate the stress to be expected in particular members of bridge structures and to determine experimentally just how massive the members had to be in order for them to carry particular loads. Problems of bridge design were no longer solved by intuition but through the application of Newtonian physics. Newton did not provide a set of rules that could be directly applied to the construction of bridges; rather he gave the bridge builder the tools for intelligent thought about bridge problems.

Psychology has had a similar impact on the practice of education. Half a century ago the teacher confronted with a child who was not learning was able to suggest little except perhaps that the child did not have the moral fortitude required to pursue his studies effectively. The teacher today immediately has a number of reasonable hypotheses about why a child is not learning. The modern teacher will question whether the child is a victim of brain damage at birth. Or whether the child comes from an environment where no value is placed on academic learning. Or whether the child has a hearing loss. All of these hypotheses, and others too, may have to be examined to find a source of the child's failure. The teacher may even seek the help of professional specialists in order to locate the source of the problem—if the source can be located. This kind of search is vastly more *intelligent* than that of the teacher near the turn of the century who might have lectured or punished the child. It is intelligent behavior that characterizes the application of knowledge derived from the scientific disciplines to problems of a practical nature. Note that the modern teacher does not have a rule-of-thumb procedure to follow when confronted with a child who does not learn. Scientific knowledge rarely, if ever, produces a simple rule for handling practical problems.

Research on learning and perception will have an impact on the audiovisual field by permitting the practitioner to make more intelligent decisions than he would otherwise make. In planning a sound-motion picture, the well-trained audiovisual specialist can ask questions about the appropriateness of the rate at which information is being communicated. He can ask whether the significant features of the visual material can be readily structured by the percipient. He can examine the narration for appropriateness of vocabulary and sentence structure. He can raise issues about the effect of using two perceptual systems rather than one. He can ask whether the conditions are such that they are most likely to attract and hold the student's attention. All of these are questions related to substantial existing knowledge in the behavioral sciences. The research worker cannot give the producer a checklist of steps to follow, but he can give him intelligent advice and criticism. As in the building of bridges, the knowledge of the scientist is not likely to produce immediate and dramatic changes in what the practitioner does, but it will affect the practitioner's entire approach to his problems.

This discussion should not be interpreted as asserting that there are not occasional discoveries which produce revolutionary changes in what the practitioner does. The discovery of X-rays did bring about a radical change in the practice of medicine. The discovery of means of producing and recoding radio waves did revolutionize communication systems. But these are notable exceptions, for the typical impact of science on practical affairs is through the impact of extensive accumulated knowledge. Generally, it is the broad background of concepts and ideas provided by science that influences the steady progress in applied fields rather than the single dramatic discovery. Educational administrators have too often looked to the research worker for some unusual discovery that will produce dramatic change in the schools. Educational research may never produce such a discovery, but research will slowly produce a body of knowledge that will change the practices of those close to the education of children. It is with the slow and steady impact of the discipline related to education that this book is concerned.

What we have been discussing up to this point is the kind of research that is commonly called "basic." In research that is called "applied," a somewhat different relationship of research to practice appears to exist. Applied research, and certainly as it has been undertaken in the audiovisual area, does tend to provide recipes for making many of the minor routine decisions that have to be made in the design and use of such materials. For example, research has shown that there is little advantage in using color in a motion picture unless the task to be learned involves color discrimination. Color does not seem to add sufficient interest value or attention-getting value to a presentation to produce any measurable effect on learning. Perhaps the only general justification for the use of color is that it provides a more pleasing esthetic experience than does black and white. The study of color versus black and white provides a useful kind of finding, but not one that has any great implications for solving any major and central issue related to the design of audiovisual materials. A number of other findings of this order of significance have emerged from applied research in the audiovisual field.

The Perceptual Systems

The traditional view of the senses was that they were a system of passive receptors dormant until exposed to the particular kind of energy, mechanical force, or chemical substance to which the particular receptor responded. According to this view, sensations were received by a passive sensory system that, in turn, transmitted impulses to the higher centers where they were interpreted. The latter operation was referred to as *perception,* and the uninterpreted inputs from the sense organs were referred to as *sensations.* Such a distinction between sensation and perception is no longer considered to have either validity or utility, and other aspects of this analysis of the sensory system have also been questioned.

Thoughtful philosophers have long speculated on how many senses should be listed in a complete inventory. Aristotle counted five and established a myth that is still widely accepted. Later attempts to compile a complete inventory generally extended the list to include at least twice as many. For example, the sensations derived from the surface of the skin were originally described as involving touch, but later it became noted that some receptors in the skin responded to temperature rather than mechanical contact. Hence, the over-all concept of touch had to be broken down into two and later into more components. In addition, deep within the body were receptor organs of unknown numbers and kinds that provided inputs to the central nervous system. Attempts to develop a complete inventory turned out to be a profitless venture. Gibson (1966) has pointed out that there is today no widely accepted list of sense modalities and that the attempt to produce one does not seem to be a useful enterprise. However, he has proposed that there are "five familiar modes of external attention" (Gibson, 1966, p. 49). It is this position that will be considered here and will be used as a structure for much of this book.

Gibson takes the position that what he calls the "external modes of attention" are not just passive systems waiting to be activated by some external source of stimulation, but rather are active exploratory systems that seek out information from the environment and are highly selective in the information they pick up. They are not "senses" in the way in which this term was used in earlier literature, but are referred to as *perceptual systems*. From the point of view of this book, they represent information systems. The list of perceptual systems includes the following five:

1. *The Basic Orienting System*. This system is centered around the vestibular organs in the inner ear that have long been known to play a central role in maintaining balance and an upright orientation to the environment. The activity of the system is immediately brought into play if the person is pushed or falls, at which time righting reflexes are evoked. The system also interacts with the visual system in that the loss of balance is also accompanied by a change in position relative to the horizon. The system maintains the body right side up to the world.

2. *The Haptic System*. This includes a complex system of receptors in the skin, joints, and muscles, and it may also be considered to include the receptors that respond to temperature. The system permits active exploration of the environment and of objects in the environment. In the exploration of an object, information derived from the receptors in the skin combines with information derived from the muscles and joints to provide a basis for the perception of shape. The muscular system is a necessary and integral part of the haptic system, for without suitable muscular activity the system could provide only the most limited information about the environment. The system does not provide passive impressions of the environment but impressions based on active exploration. The system does not wait for the environment to stimulate it; rather, it acts upon the environment.

3. *The Taste-Smell System*. This again is an active system that explores the nature of solid, liquid, and gaseous material. It is a highly specialized exploratory system.

4. *The Visual System*. Although the organ of vision is thought of as the eye, the perceptual system also includes a complex muscular arrangement that permits an optical search of the environment. Even

the large muscles of the limbs play a part in visual search, as when a person turns his body to bring into view the source of a noise behind him. Although the retina provides the receptor mechanism, it is only one component of the visual perceptual system. Without the other components, the system would be limited to a relatively useless role of passive reception.

5. *The Auditory System.* The central organ of the auditory system is a mechanical analyzer of vibratory events in the middle ear. Muscle systems result in an orientation to sound sources and permit the picking up of faint signals. Unlike the case of vision, the reception of sound signals is not highly dependent upon the physical orientation of the receiver, though reception may be improved if the ears are oriented for maximum sensitivity to the source.

The five perceptual systems do not include all of the sensory inputs to the nervous system. Each is a complex system involving receptor and muscles related to the positioning of the body. The systems are not just means by which the phenomena of the outside world impress themselves on the living creature, but are also systems capable of seeking out information and, in some cases, of even scanning the environment for signals of significance.

After making this classification of the perceptual systems and emphasizing their complexity, Gibson goes on to point out that training can produce enhanced skill in the utilization of any of these systems. Such training does not produce improved use of the sense organ as such, but improvement in the functioning of the complex system in which it is located.

Since education places heavy emphasis on the use of the visual and the auditory perceptual systems, most of this book will be devoted to a discussion of how these systems receive and utilize environment-derived information. Some educators have also wanted to give equal emphasis to the haptic system, but since this system requires that the learner come into close physical contacts with objects, learning through the haptic system cannot be readily used in a group situation. In the Montessori method, children are given many experiences communicated through the haptic system, as when pieces of sandpaper are provided and the children are to sort them according to degree of roughness. Such an experience could be used to develop such concepts as *rougher than, roughest, least rough,* as well as the concept of an ordered scale. However, each pupil must virtually have his own set of materials, for little value would be achieved by the teacher demonstrating the arrangement of the pieces of sandpaper in order, and using language to show the use of the concepts to be learned. The direct contact required in the use of the haptic system limits the extent to which it can be utilized in an educational setting at the present time. There is every reason to believe that the haptic system has the same potential for transmitting information as have the auditory and the visual systems. The extraordinarily effective performance of such well-educated examples of humanity as Helen Keller shows very clearly how a highly sophisticated conception of the environment can be developed *almost* entirely through the haptic system. The latter statement is worded in a qualified way since Helen Keller did have vision and hearing during infancy—a fact which may have been enormously important to her subsequent effective use of the haptic system. It is conceivable that even without the early auditory and visual experiences Helen Keller might still have reached her high level of intellectual accomplishment.

Redundancy in Perceptual Information

Sometimes, when a test is given to school children, the test administrator reads the directions aloud while the pupils read them at the same time from the printed text. The information coming into the pupils through the visual and the auditory systems is said to be *redundant*. That is to say, both sets of information have exactly the same consequences in terms of what the pupil does. The equivalence of the spoken and the printed word is taken for granted, and yet one is transmitted through vibrations in the atmosphere and the other through light. Now let us consider another case where Gibson points out that the stimuli are roughly equivalent though not to the same degree.

A person standing near a log fire sees the glow of the flames, hears the crackling of the embers, feels the impact of the heat on his skin, and smells the tar and distillates in the smoke. All of these inputs are partially equivalent, much as speech and printed words are equivalent, in that each indicates the presence of a fire. A blind and deaf man can be just as certain of the presence of a fire as a seeing and hearing man. The inputs are not completely equivalent in that one also carries with it more varied information about the fire than does another. Through vision, one can identify more than the mere presence or absence of a fire; one can identify the color of the flame, the contours of the various logs, and other features. The equivalence is only complete when the task is that of identifying the presence or absence of a fire. In a manner of speaking, one can obtain the same knowledge about the environment through the different perceptual systems, and in this way the environment can be mastered despite severe sensory limitations, as in the case of the blind and deaf Helen Keller. Nevertheless, the full *experience* of the environment requires that redundant information be experienced through the different perceptual systems. However, fullness of experience is a different matter from the informative value of experience.

The redundancy of information probably makes objects more readily recognizable if they can be recognized through many different redundant cues, and a case can perhaps be made for including redundant information in educational experiences. The audiovisual experts have long had the notion that a full education somehow required that redundant information be introduced. Thus, for example, it is considered better to expose a child to the visual experience of a sheep, the auditory experience of the typical "baa," and the tactual experience of the soft and silky texture of the sheep, than simply to show the child a picture of a sheep. Why the city child should have to be able to identify the sound of a sheep's bleat or the texture of fleece is an interesting point to raise. The audiovisual experts might say that only a child who had these experiences had a "full" concept of a sheep, but the fact is that the city child is likely to have only visual contact with sheep while driving on highways, and is very unlikely to have to identify a sheep by means other than the visual. The auditory and haptic information about sheep would appear to have virtually no utility.

A much stronger argument for presenting the entire range of information through different perceptual systems is that children like to explore their environments in every way and generally prefer a full rather than a restricted kind of exploration. This argument is persuasive. It really comes down to the idea that the exploration of the environment through all the senses is a preferred way of exploration in the young human of, say, elementary-school age. Children naturally touch and handle and look at and sometimes even taste objects. Merely to be allowed to view an object held up by the teacher is much less satisfying than a situation in which a much fuller exploration is possible. For this reason, one is led to the position that despite the lack of utility, the introduction of redundant information about the same object through different perceptual systems may be a desirable way to proceed in an educational setting, even though it does not result in the learning of more useful information.

Man as an Information System

Although man can be seen in many different lights, he is to be studied through the medium of this book as a system deriving information from the environment and selectively storing aspects of that information for later utilization. This is not to deny the existence of many other facets of man's complex relationship to his environment, but this book is restricted to the one aspect that has to do with man obtaining and storing information. The school may attempt to develop the student's ability to relate to his environment in many different ways by providing him materials to model and mold, by presenting him with displays that arouse feeling and emotion, by giving him the protection and support he needs particularly in the early years, and by giving him numerous other sources of stimulation that serve some significant purpose other than that of providing information. Although one may recognize the importance of all the different ways in which man may relate to his environment, his survival depends in a central and crucial way on his ability to receive, utilize, and store information. It is this central aspect of man's intelligence that this book explores.

Information and Perception

As perception has come to be regarded as an information-processing sequence of events, the term *information* has been widely introduced, often with a variety of meanings within the same statement. In a popular sense, it is quite obvious that perception has the function of providing information *about* the environment; but information about the environment is different from the information *in* the environment. The environment has to have some structure before it can be said to provide any information at all. If the field of vision consisted of a field in which small specks of light appeared at random anywhere in the field, the visual world would be providing no information in the technical sense of the term. On the other hand, a visual world in which the events do not occur at random, but in which there is structure, is a world that provides information. Parallel statements could be made about the auditory world. If the latter were to consist of a jumble of randomly occurring sounds, the environment would provide no information at all. The auditory environment does provide information in that most sound is not random. In speech, sound occurs in definite patterns that can be identified, and in music, the patterning of sound is crucial to the production of esthetic effects. The environment does provide information in that the inputs to the senses are not random inputs of light and sound, but are patterned inputs. If the inputs were random, then the inputs would be referred to as *noise* (but this is not noise in a popular sense of the term).

One can speak of information as being related to structure, in contrast to randomness. This is one concept of information that derives largely from the concept of entropy—a measure indicating the disorder in a closed system derived from the field of thermodynamics. This is the most fundamental of all concepts of information and provides a useful way of viewing the information content of the environment. The greater the order and the less the randomness of events in the environment the greater is the potential source of information. But this is not the only concept of information that is of use in helping to understand the perceptual systems and their relationship to the environment. More commonly one thinks of information as involving a transmission in a communication system with a sender and a receiver and a set of energy changes through which the information is transmitted from the one to the other. Within such a framework, information is defined as that which reduces uncertainty at the receiver end of the system. In this model, as in the lack-of-disorder concept of information, random inputs to the system represent a state of affairs in which there is an absence of information, that is to say, an input of noise.

Let us consider further what is meant by the reduction of uncertainty at the receiver end. Uncertainty refers to a decision-making situation in which the choice of alternative can be made only on a random basis until information arrives. The amount of information needed to reduce uncertainty in a two-choice situation defines one bit of information. Thus, in a situation in which action is to take place and in which there are two possible alternative actions, the information that determines which of the two courses is to be followed is designated as a bit of information. This concept of information and the role of information in decision making applies to machines as well as to man. A computer may go through a program up to a certain point where a decision has to be made whether to terminate the analysis or to extend it further. One bit of information is needed in order for the machine to make the decision. Random events arriving at the receiver do not reduce uncertainty and do not represent information but are what is termed noise. Most messages arrive contaminated with a certain amount of noise. What we are discussing here is classical information theory which enables us to identify information and to contrast it with the noninformational inputs to the senses, even though classical information theory was developed as a means of understanding electrical problems rather than biological.

Mention has already been made of the fact that one typically thinks of communication as involving a sender and a receiver and that the energy involved in the communication generally undergoes many changes when it passes from the sender to the receiver. These changes in the energy involve the *coding* of the information. Call a friend on the telephone, and the message you send to him is first coded into air vibrations which are transmitted to the microphone where they are then recoded into electrical changes that travel along the line until they are reconverted into air vibrations by means of your friend's telephone receiver. Your friend receives these vibrations and has to decode them in order to understand your message. The transmission of information is always a complex chain of events in which the information becomes encoded in various forms. All information about the environment is coded physiologically by the receptors into sequences of nerve impulses, but the information is also later converted psychologically into new codes before it evokes responses of recognition, or other responses, in the person who is the receiver. Much of the incoming information that is handled by the perceptual systems is probably coded into words before it is stored or otherwise used. Other incoming information is coded into other forms that in some way represent objects in the external world. Whatever activity in the nervous system represents imagery would represent one form of coding of information.

Inputs may be classified in many different ways. One classification depends upon the nature of the physical stimuli involved, such as light or mechanical touch. Another classification already considered is that of signal and noise. Still another classification, proposed by Knowlton (1966) for vision, categorizes inputs into *iconic* and *digital*. A picture that in some way physically resembles an object would be considered to be in the iconic category, while a printed word or other symbol would represent a digital input. A similar classification could be developed for auditory inputs. Knowlton also has a further system for classifying all iconic inputs.

The way in which information from the external world becomes transformed internally into a useful decision system is quite crucial to understanding why sometimes some inputs are more useful than others in promoting successful learning or action. Later in this book use will be made of a system similar to that developed by Knowlton, but it will be applied to the classification of information held in the memory system, rather than to inputs of information.

Perception as the Search for Constancies

Let us consider further the development of the perception and storage of information related to the constancies in the environment. Nearly all adults have the experience from time to time of listening to a language with which they are totally unfamiliar. After they have listened for a few minutes, one can ask them, "What did you hear?" They are likely to reply that all they could hear was a jumble of sounds, and the chances are that they will not be able to repeat a single sound element. Yet the language was not just a jumble of unorganized sound. To the listener familiar with it, the language provided a structured system of sounds. To such a knowledgeable listener, the sound elements (or *phonemes,* as they are called) could have been clearly identified, and the language would have been recognized as an ordered system of phonemes. In addition, groups of phonemes would have been recognized as constituting particular words, and the arrangement of the words would have been recognized as representing a system of rules referred to as the grammar of the language. These regularities, or *constancies,* as they are called in the flow of the language, would be completely unrecognized in the person unfamiliar with it, but through just listening to the language some of the regularities would slowly become evident. The commonly occurring sounds would begin to stand out first and then, slowly, the other less frequently occurring sounds would begin to emerge. The language teacher helps the pupil become aware of these *constancies* in a new language by emphasizing particular sounds and groups of sounds. When these are readily recognized, the teacher then adds new sounds to be recognized. The speed with which a particular sound or group of sounds can be recognized depends upon the frequency of exposure to it. By the provision of extensive practice in recognizing sounds, the rate of recognition is gradually speeded up until words can be recognized with the rapidity necessary for slow speech, and later fast speech, to be comprehended.

While most of us have the experience of having our auditory world filled with the unfamiliar, few ever have the same experience in the visual area. One is readily tempted to generalize that if it were possible to have a brand-new experience in a wholly novel visual environment, that the perceiver would find himself confronted with the same lack of structure as that which confronts him when he first hears a language entirely different from his own. Such a generalization from the auditory perceptual system to the visual does seem justified. This is brought home by the reports of adults who, through a corneal graft, gain vision for the first time. Adults who have this experience report that they are surrounded by a confusing visual world, but it is not a wholly unorganized visual world. There are objects which stand out as things, even though the things have no identity or recognizable attributes. Thus when such a patient has held up in front of him a square piece of board, he can state that there is an object there, but he cannot state what the object is, and cannot even identify it as having corners. The identification of "thinghood" is different from the identification of things with specific properties. The first of these is primitive and unlearned; the second is a product of experience.

Just as the adult slowly learns to identify the constancies in a foreign language, so does the child come to recognize constancies in the visual world. The frequent appearance of the mother's face in different positions and at different distances makes that face one of the first objects to be identified and discriminated from other objects. Food objects also come to be identified at an early age. Soon, such significant parts of the environment are readily recognized regardless of position or distance, just as spoken words are recognized regardless of whether they are spoken softly or loudly, with a male voice or a female voice, or with many other variations. Whatever remains constant regardless of such variation is that which the child has to learn to identify with his perceptual system. Perceptual learning in early childhood is partly learning to identify the frequently occurring constancies of the environment.

The visual inputs are structured by the boundaries, direction of slope, color reflectance, and other properties of the environment that in turn provide some structure to the visual images representing them. Civilized environments built by man generally provide greater structure in terms of gross form than do highly primitive environments.

Contrast the visual environment of a man sitting in a room furnished in a modern style with the environment of a man in the jungle. The jungle scene involves a great amount of inconsequential detail that functions perceptually as just so much visual noise, while the civilized environment provides a high degree of structure.

Sound is structured in terms of frequency and intensity, but the important information is generally carried by the frequency ratios. Thus a sound pattern can be dropped half an octave or raised half an octave but still be identified as the same pattern. It is not the actual frequencies that count but the relationship of the frequencies to one another, that is to say, the ratios of the different frequencies involved.

The perceptual systems take information from the environment. The wealth of information that reaches the retina of the eye or the cochlea of the ear does not represent the quantity of information that is needed at the higher levels of the perceptual system for maintaining the relationship of the organism to the environment. Perceptual learning involves the identification of those constancies in the environment that provide information of crucial value and the suppression of those sources of environmental information that have relatively little value. Of primary importance are those aspects of the environment that represent constancies—that is, those aspects of the environment that have unchanging significant features for the organism living in it.

The Information Capacity of a Perceptual System

One can view the retina, optic nerve, relay ganglia, and occipital lobe of the brain (that part of the cortex which has specifically visual functions) as forming an information-transmission system. Such a system can be considered to have a channel capacity for handling information, just as a radio beam can be considered to have a certain capacity for handling information. One can think of the retina and the optic nerve for conducting visual information as having a basic capacity for handling information, but this capacity may be different from the actual amount of information transmitted by a particular message. Consider, for example, the analogy of a television channel, which has a very large capacity for handling information, about 5 million bits per second. When this large-capacity system is used in the early hours of the morning just to indicate whether one is tuned to Channel 2 or Channel 5, the message communicated carries only one bit of information; that is to say, it enables one to decide in a two-choice situation which of the two channels is being tuned in. Thus a system with a large channel capacity of 5 million bits per second may be used to carry only one bit of information. Much the same can happen in the utilization of vision—a communication system that has probably roughly the same channel capacity as a television channel. This large-capacity optical system can be used to handle messages which carry as little as one bit of information. Indeed, much of the complicated system of vision is utilized for the making of decisions that involve only a single bit of information. It is of interest to point out that many other situations in daily life also involve a very complicated set of mechanisms to produce, in the final analysis, a single bit of information. For example, in presidential elections, the entire electoral machinery and the total activities of millions of voters ultimately lead in most cases to a decision between two presidential candidates—a decision in a two-choice situation involving one bit of information.

The perceptual systems provide some direct information about ongoing events in the world. The perceptual systems also pick up coded information that provides very indirect means of knowing the environment. Gibson (1966) refers to the latter perceptual information as providing knowledge *about* the environment, in contrast to knowledge *of* the environment. If a person hears his name called, the fact that he hears the *sound* of his name indicates that he has knowledge *of* his environment, but the recognition of his name, and the fact that the calling of it demands some response on his part, indicates that he has knowledge *about* the environment.

Even the simplest information about the environment requires the use of some set of rules for interpretation. For example, we see a man across the street as a very small image on the retinas at the back of our eyes because he is quite a distance away. The man does not look small, even though the retinal images are small, because we have rules for interpreting such information. Indeed, he will look just as big as the man standing next to us. In this case the rules for interpreting the information from the environment are so well ingrained in our systems that we do not even realize they exist nor that our perception is dependent upon them.

There is no clear line of demarcation between direct and uncoded information and coded or symbolic information. If one hears a cry of pain, the cry is, in a sense, crude and uncoded information derived directly from the environment, but it also comes close to being symbolic information in that the cry, in itself, represents a person suffering. It is much more than just a sound that is recognized by the perceptual system. It is also a symbol in that it arouses expectancies and images of the cry-related source. The difference between a piece of coded information and a piece of direct information of the environment resides in the complexity of the rules involved in the interpretation.

Coded information is not necessarily information given in words. A picture of a man with a bright incandescent bulb glowing in his head is often used to portray a man who has just achieved some great insight. Such a picture might be interpreted at the simplest level as that of a man with an electric bulb burning in his head. But such an interpretation would be wrong, having failed to use the information correctly because the rules applied in interpreting the material were inappropriate. Such a picture has to be interpreted in terms of a much more complex set of rules which will permit the person to recognize that it is not the physical features of the light bulb that are crucial but the verbal equivalence of light and understanding. Many failures to interpret information correctly stem from the use of incorrect rules for the interpretation of the perceptual information.

The rules that the adult has learned for interpreting coded information are so much taken for granted that it is sometimes hard to realize that the young may find the same information difficult to understand because they have not yet learned the rules. For a man who uses maps, the procedures for interpreting them are so clear and obvious that it is difficult to believe that the most difficult section of basic training for the army recruit to master is the section on map reading. A table of organization consisting of little boxes filled with the names of positions and incumbents is quite unintelligible to the uninitiated. Metaphors, analogies, and other figures of speech represent subtle means of coding information where the perceiver must select the right rule in order to extract the information provided. When one misses the point of a conversation, it is often the result of a failure to apply the appropriate rule in the interpretation of a figure of speech.

Information Inputs and Knowledge

A distinction must be made between information inputs and knowledge. Knowledge is coded information. If I look at an orange and experience the roundness and orange color and the citrus aroma, I am receiving information, and any very young child can not only receive this information but can also store it and utilize it on later occasions. After many such encounters, one can demonstrate by experimental techniques more complicated than can be described here that the child recognizes the orange and also recognizes the specific attributes of the fruit. The child can be said to have received and stored information pertaining to the orange, but the child does not have knowledge in the sense in which the term knowledge is used here. He would have knowledge if the information about the orange had been translated within him into words. Only when the information has been thus encoded into words does one speak of the child as having knowledge. Thus, as the word is used here, a man can have knowledge but a chimpanzee cannot. Knowledge that has been thus coded may be stored outside or inside the individual. If it is stored external to himself in books or manuscript form, the knowledge can be retrieved by whoever is familiar with the encoding and decoding system. If one reads that a certain fruit is orange in color, one has to know the sensory experience represented by the word *orange* for this particular word to have meaning. Not all words will have a simple relation to sensory experience, and many involve very complicated encoding.

Chapter 2

The Nervous System, Information Processing, and Information Coding

The study of man as an information system can be pursued by two rather different approaches. One involves the study of the anatomy and physiology of the nervous system and related structures; the other engages in research on behavior. The two approaches are extraordinarily intertwined. There are physiologists who have derived their basic ideas for research from experiments conducted by psychologists, and many psychologists seek suggestions from the physiologist. The assumption is always that the combined partnership of these two disciplines will produce a single and unified body of knowledge about the common problems with which they are involved. Our approach here is to begin by considering the physiological and neurological basis of information processing and then to turn later to the psychological contributions to these same problems.

The Nervous System

All nervous systems, except those in the simplest multicellular organisms are built of the same kind of units—the nerve cells. These come in many different forms, but they all have cell bodies that play a crucial role in the nutritive processes of the cell as a whole. In one common type of nerve cell, illustrated in Figure 1, there is a long filament extending from one end—the *axon*—which may extend for several feet. At the other end are branching filaments referred to as *dendrites*. The long axon permits the conduction of nerve impulses from one part of the body to another. The axons are the long lines of the body's communication system. Other cells have no dendrites, and still others have a double extension from one end which spans the distance from a sense organ at one end to a point within the central nervous system at the other.

The axon of a nerve cell is covered by a myelin sheath which has insulating properties that separate it from other axons of other nerve cells. The nerve impulses that travel down the axon are not like

19

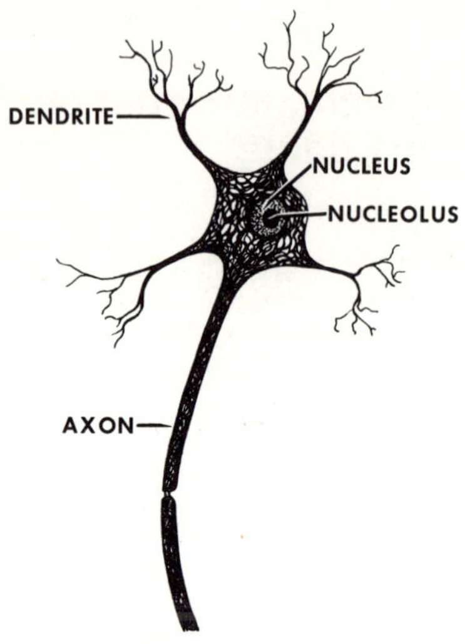

Figure 1. A common type of nerve cell.

electrical impulses in a circuit, but they do have electrical properties and can be picked up with appropriate electronic equipment. The rate of conduction of the nerve impulse varies considerably. In some nerve cells it may be as high as 400 feet per second and in others only 3 feet per second, a speed that ranges from that of a racing car to that of a slow walk. In the typical nerve cell, equipped with dendrites and an axon, the nerve impulse always travels in the same direction from dendrites to axon and then down the axon and away from the nerve cell.

The membrane that surrounds the nerve cell and its extensions is continuous and unbroken and makes the cell a single and separate living unit. The membrane keeps each cell separate from every other, and never is there continuity between the interior of one cell and the interior of another. The nervous system is *not* like a pipe network in which the fluids can flow from any one component into other components, but rather it consists of a large number of separate units, each of which has its own membrane that separates it from all other similar units. Nevertheless, there are places where the axon of one cell comes into close proximity with the dendrites of another. These locations are referred to as *synapses*. The nervous system also contains other cells, known as *glial* cells, which have unknown functions.

The number of cells in the human nervous system is about 11 billion. There are more nerve cells in a single human nervous system than there are people in the world. A single nerve cell in the brain may have hundreds of synapses relating it to other nerve cells. The complexity of the system is difficult to conceptualize, and the task of unraveling its mysteries is not made easier by the fact that a living brain has about the same consistency as that of tapioca pudding. Only after a brain has been hardened in formalin and then stained is it possible to study the microscopic anatomical detail of the system.

The synapses can vary in their ability to transmit or not to transmit impulses from one nerve cell to another. Under some conditions, the transmission is facilitated; and under others, inhibited. It is probable that all synapses can have both facilitative and inhibitory functions. The fact that the synapse is a place where change can occur and that changes can either block or facilitate the transmission of a signal suggests that this may be the location where information is stored. In other words, the suggestion is that the synapse is the seat of memory. Despite the fact that this proposal is very attractive, and there are no data to show that it is unsound, direct evidence is lacking to show that whatever is learned is stored at the synapse. Alternative hypotheses have also been suggested. One of these is that information is stored in particular molecules through a modification of molecular structure. The alternative hypotheses are generally less plausible than the hypothesis that information is stored at the synapse, though storage at that point may involve molecular change. The number of synapses seems to be sufficiently large to provide the necessary storage capacity, particularly in view of the fact that a single cell in the cortex of the brain may have hundreds of synapses relating it to very large numbers of other nerve cells.

The synapses function like on-off switches. Hence, if information is stored at the synapses, it is stored by setting a large number of on-off switches. One can easily imagine how this could be done. Consider one of those brightly lit Broadway displays urging one to buy SKULL cigarettes. The word SKULL is spelled out in lights by setting a large number of switches that turn on or off the appropriate light bulbs in the display. In a sense, the positions of the switches store the information announced to the world through the display sign. If the switches were set in different positions, then different information would come out of the display. The display could also be set to provide a picture of a skull, rather than the word, but this would involve either a different setting of the same switches or the setting of a different set of switches. Information of all sorts—pictorial, verbal, and other kinds too—can be stored in a set of on-off switches.

Nerve cells function in very much the same way over almost the entire range of living organisms. The situation is analogous to the use of transistors in computers. Such transistors are essentially the same regardless of whether they are in the simplest kind of computer that turns traffic lights on or off or in giant facilities designed to solve the most complex problems that man has ever attacked. The fact that nearly all nervous systems are built out of the same basic kind of unit opens up many approaches to the study of the nervous system which would not be feasible if man had a completely unique system for handling information about his environment, a system that differed in its components from that found in other creatures.

The similarity of nerve cells in different organisms permits the physiologist to explore some of the simpler functions of nervous processes in simpler organisms. At least a part of our knowledge of reception processes has been derived from organisms in which the entire visual reception system consists of just a few cells. The exploration of more complex levels of information analysis has involved mammals in which events in the transmission and analysis centers have been studied through the implantation of electrodes from which records are made of electrical changes in those centers. An illustration of this kind of work is found in research on the conduction of auditory information from the receptor organs in the ear to the higher centers of the brain. When sound of appreciable intensity reaches the ear, the receptors are stimulated and discharge impulses up the auditory nerve. The physiologist can study the relationship of the frequency of these impulses to the intensity of sound and thus begin to understand how sound waves are "coded" into nervous impulses. Even more important is the fact that the physiologist can trace these nervous impulses through the various relay stations and find out some of the conditions under which they reach the higher levels of the brain and the conditions under which they are blocked at one relay station or another. One does not *hear* all the sounds that are received by the ear. One does not, for example, hear the familiar tick of the grandfather's clock. The physiologist is able to trace within the nervous system the conduction of auditory information and can identify, in the case of subhumans, the particular relay point where auditory information is blocked when the animal is distracted by other sources of information.

Although the human nervous system is made up of elements very much like those in the nervous systems of other advanced, but subhuman forms of life, there is a limit to the extent to which one can generalize about man's nervous system from the study of the systems of simpler creatures. In some areas, the comparative physiologist is safe in making generalizations from simpler to more complex species. For example, the metabolism of sugar in man is essentially the same as the metabolism of sugar in dogs, and the study of the dog is of enormous value in providing understanding of disturbances of sugar metabolism in man. The metabolic systems of the dog and man are essentially the same. However, if one were to attempt to generalize to man findings of research on the nervous system of the dog, one would run into difficulties. The reason is that the nervous system of the dog does not have some of the structures found in the brain of man, who has, among other unique features, structures related to speech. Although much can be found out about the detailed functioning of nerve cells through research on lower organisms, such studies tell us little about the complex functions particularly of the higher centers of the brain of man.

Inputs of Information to the Nervous System

The sensory system which provides necessary knowledge of conditions both inside and outside the body is a specialized part of the nervous system consisting of *transducers,* that is, sense organs, transmission systems, and information-analysis systems. Transducer is an engineering term that refers to a device used for changing one form of energy into another. The cells of the retina of the eye are transducers in that they change light energy into a series of nerve impulses in the optic nerve. Other transducers in the ear change the energy present in vibrations in the reverbertory components of the ear into energy represented by impulses in the auditory nerve. The receptors are structures that respond to particular energy changes and produce a characteristic pattern of nerve impulses.

Information about the outside world is received through a system of sensitive cells located mainly, but not entirely, near the boundary surfaces of the body. Some of the receptors, such as those involved in providing information about the position of the limbs, are deeply embedded within the body. Fragmentary knowledge of how one manages to receive information about the outside world has long been available. As early as 1604, Kepler identified the retina of the eye as a structure which somehow was able to pick up and register a picture of the outside world, but it required the development of the microscope and staining techniques for the nerve structures involved to be mapped out and identified. Although much has been learned since the time of Kepler, there are still very large blank areas in our knowledge concerning the reception process.

The nerve fibers that conduct the sensory information to the higher centers of the nervous system are called the *afferent fibers*. They do not proceed individually and separately from the receptor to the spinal cord and then to the higher centers; rather, they are gathered into bundles which appear as silvery white cords when dissected. One such bundle enters the spinal cord on each side for each body segment. A body segment corresponds roughly to each of the vertebrae in the spinal column—the bony column which encases the spinal cord. Between each pair of vertebrae a nerve enters on each side carrying impulses from receptors within the particular body segment. In addition, other nerves, including the auditory and the optic nerves, enter the central nervous system at locations beneath the main mass of the brain.

The path of communication between the receptor and the brain is a nerve tract, but it does not consist of continuous nerve filaments as in a telephone cable. The continuity of the tract is broken, generally at two points, by relay stations known as *nuclei*. In a nucleus the fibers coming from the direction of the receptor terminate, and the nerve impulses are passed on to new fibers attached to new cells. The nuclei consist of nerve cells and synapses. Only the most incomplete information is available concerning the function of the nuclei. One fact seems fairly certain: that impulses traveling up a particular sensory tract can be partially blocked at a nucleus through activity of the higher centers. Such a mechanism can account for the fact that one may not hear the radio in the next room when one is completely absorbed in reading a book. Under such a condition, the higher centers *could* conceivably block the information arriving from the ears through producing a blocking effect at a relay point between the ear and the cortex. There is, in fact, some evidence that such an inhibitory condition does actually occur. Another possible function of the nuclei is that of information analysis. So far there is not much direct evidence to support such a function, though some neurophysiologists maintain that some information is analyzed at subcortical levels. A third possible function is that of information storage, but here again there is little evidence to support the hypothesis that information storage at such levels is possible.

The spinal cord is a connecting system that links sense organs with the higher centers and also links the higher centers with the muscles and glands through which action can be effected and maintained. In other words, impulses travel up the spinal cord to transmit information from the receptor organs, and impulses travel down the cord to produce muscular and glandular responses. The spinal cord also has functions in the relaying of nerve impulses, and some reflexes are handled entirely through activity within the spinal cord. A living creature in whom the spinal cord has been severed will, after recovery from the ensuing state of shock, show reflexes below the level of the severed spinal cord. Sometimes such reflexes will be manifested in an accentuated form because the inhibiting and controlling effect of the brain can no longer operate.

A great number of different techniques have been developed for the study of how the brain works. The most obvious approach would be that of dissecting it, bit by bit, and from a study of its structure making deductions about how it works, but this technique has not been very successful partly because of the extraordinary complexity and compactness of the tissues involved. The mapping out of the positions and interrelationships of a few billion neurones is an impossible task in itself. Also, each human brain probably differs from every other in minute detail. Some of the earliest productive studies involved relating changes in behavior to the destruction of brain tissue produced by tumors. Later, as surgical techniques developed, it became possible to question patients parts of whose brain had been exposed and then electrically stimulated. The vivid visual experiences produced by stimulating some areas toward the rear and side of the brain indicated that such areas have functions related to vision. Experimental techniques have also been developed on animals, and much research has involved the effect of producing damage at particular locations and studying the effects on behavior. Sometimes this research has involved the study of the effect of severing particular nerve tracts or of damaging particular nuclei. In addition, studying the effect produced by drugs applied to particular brain localities has also turned out to be a very useful technique. Some of the newer techniques involve the electronic recording of what is taking place in specific nerve fibers. Electrodes have been developed which are so thin that they can be inserted in such a way that they come into contact with a single nerve fiber or with single cells.

Considerable caution has to be exercised in generalizing from brain studies of the subhuman to understanding the brain and the behavior of the human. The subhuman brain may have far more built-in mechanisms for handling information about the environment than does the human. The effective functioning of the human brain is highly dependent upon learning and, hence, requires extensive experience before being able to cope with even simple aspects of the environment.

The Brain

The human brain is a structure of enormous complexity, only the gross details of which can be described here. In the embryo, the nervous system begins as a hollow tube of cells lying along the back. The lower part of this tube becomes the spinal cord—the main trunk line for conducting information from the body to the higher centers and for transmitting information to the muscles and action systems. As the embryo develops, massive development takes place at one end of this tube of cells to become the large organ known as the brain. This large mass of nervous tissue remains continuous with the spinal cord.

Figures 2 and 3 show a human brain from two different positions. Figure 2 shows the brain as it would be seen from the side after it has been removed from its bony case. In Figure 3 the brain has been sliced down the middle with a cut that would pass through the middle of the forehead and down the back of the head. It thus gives a view of the interior of the brain and brain stem as seen in such a section.

Let us first consider the view shown in Figure 3. The largest mass of tissue shown in this figure is one of the two *cerebral hemispheres*. These are the most evident organs and represent what is described in common terms as the brain. They involve as much as 80 per cent of the tissues in the higher centers and have functions associated with all higher mental processes, the storage of information, and the control

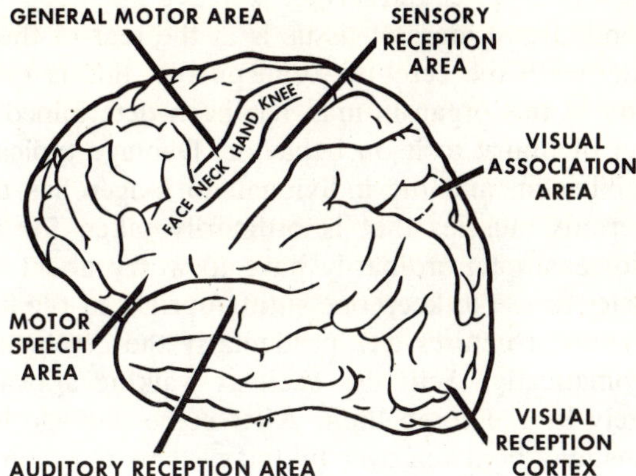

Figure 2. Side view of the human brain.

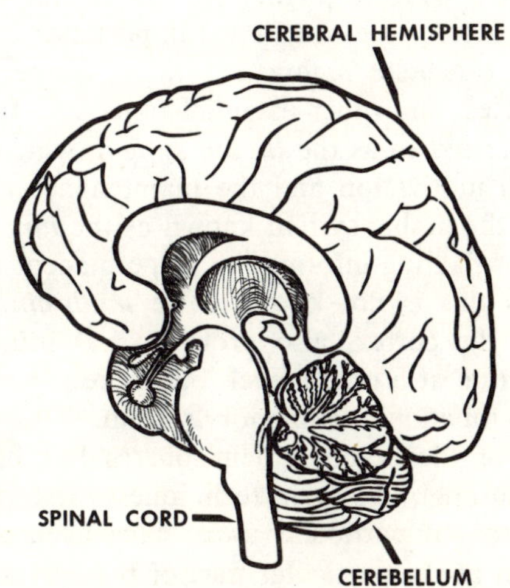

Figure 3. View of a midsection of the brain cut from the top of the head downward.

of voluntary movement. The effective functioning of these organs is highly dependent upon the amount of surface area, which is large as a result of the way in which the surface is folded into deep troughs.

The second-largest mass of tissue is at the rear of the brain and is tucked underneath the cerebral hemispheres; this is the *cerebellum.* The function of this organ in man has been determined from studies of the effect of injury to it on behavior. Damage typically results in loss of equilibrium, and the individual no longer has the automatic control over his muscles that is ordinarily taken for granted. One does not, for example, ordinarily have to worry about the matter of which muscles to use to keep one sitting upright at the lunch counter, because various structures and particularly the cerebellum take care of this automatically. Activities such as walking appear to be controlled largely by the cerebellum. After some damage to this organ, the functions may be taken over by the systems that handle voluntary control.

In the upper part of the spinal cord is found a diffuse mass of tissue known as the *reticular activating system,* which plays a fundamental role in maintaining wakefulness and a state of alertness. It also plays an important role in phenomena related to attention and motivation.

Most of the structures through which the spinal cord and brain stem are connected with the higher centers cannot be seen on these figures. These structures are of extreme importance for regulating and maintaining vital processes such as breathing, temperature regulation, sleep-activity cycles, and other essential functions. In addition, there are structures referred to as the *limbic system,* which appear to have much to do with motivation and the maintenance of states of vigilance. A part of the limbic system known as the *hippocampus,* seems to be essential for fixating information in permanent memory, though just how it does this is not known. The *midbrain,* connecting the brain stem with the cortex, also probably has information-analysis systems that operate at a crude level, but there is no evidence that it has any ability to function as a memory system.

The function of the cerebral hemispheres has been explored in human subjects through two main techniques. First, persons in whom lesions have destroyed particular areas have been studied to determine the function of the particular part of the cortex affected by the lesions. Second, patients whose brain has been partly exposed for surgery can have particular locations electrically stimulated and they can be asked to report what effect this stimulation has on their mental processes.

Through these kinds of techniques, a number of conclusions can be drawn about the function of the surface areas of the cerebral cortex. An important finding is that most of the cortex appears to have what may be termed *nonspecific* functions; that is, the areas involved do not have any particular sensory function or functions related to the control of particular movements. They do presumably perform such activities as storing information either temporarily or permanently, and they are the areas involved in the retrieval of stored information and in the processes related to decision making.

A second point to note is that some areas of the cortex are closely related to the functioning of particular sensory systems. For example, a small area at the rear of each cerebral lobe and the related area tucked in between the two lobes has to do with visual information. The latter parts of the cerebral lobes are known as the *occipital lobes.* Other well-located areas have to do with auditory reception and the reception of what is called *somesthetic sensations,* that is, information from the sense organs located in the skin. In addition, some areas have to do specifically with the control of movements. One area, known as *Broca's area,* has to do with the control of speech, but other areas also have other specialized speech functions. A person who has damage to Broca's area will be unable to speak even though he can understand everything that is said to him. A strip of tissue on either side of the cortex that extends roughly from the top of the head to a point near the top of each ear, has to do with the control of movement of various parts of the body.

A point of particular interest in connection with the present discussion is that most of the so-called association areas are not tied to any particular perceptual system or sensory input, except indirectly. The more important aspects of human memory are probably in a verbal form. Indeed, there is an increasing volume of evidence that visual information is not likely to be remembered in precise detail unless it is coded into words. The words "a ball of polished lucite 3 inches in diameter" record much more precise information about this object than does a vague visual image of the ball. Man's ability to code sensory inputs into words and to remember the words may well account for most of his extraordinary feats of memory. Memories coded into words permit him to have a storage system of information in which all information is coded and stored in the same form regardless of whether the original information came to him through the visual, auditory, or haptic system. More about this topic will be said later.

Some areas of the cortex seem to be tied to exploratory behavior. The *parietal areas,* for example, seem to have functions related to exploration with the haptic and visual systems. Damage to this area results in the avoidance of such exploration and a withdrawal from the environment. Furthermore, impairment of the *temporal lobes* results in difficulties in visual recognition.

Another important point to note about the cortex of the brain is that, in the adult, damage to one particular area does not result in the loss of specific memories. In other words, particular pieces of information one has learned are not stored in particular locations, as they are in the case of a computer. The same piece of information may well be stored in different localities, or it may be stored in a network of cells and synapses, thereby permitting recall of the item of information even when a part of the network has been destroyed.

Coding at the Receptor Level

An understanding of the information-transmission process in the human organism requires knowledge of the ways in which the information received is coded at the receptors. Except for the chemical senses, information is received by the receptors in the form of energy changes or continuous levels of energy impact. It is well known that each receptor is constructed to be particularly sensitive to certain energy changes rather than to others—the receptors on the retina being particularly responsive to changes involving light energy; touch receptors in the skin, to mild mechanical impact; and so forth. However, these receptors will respond to other forms of energy. A blow to the eye may trigger the light-sensitive cells of the retina so that one "sees stars." All the information which the organism receives about its environment, either internal or external, comes through energy impact at the receptor level or through chemical interaction in the case of smell and taste. The information reaching the receptors is changed in form there, before it is transmitted to the higher centers of the brain. This change in the form of information is referred to as *coding.* Coding involves a change in the nature of the energy transmitting the signal, as when information conveyed by light is changed at the retina to an electrochemical activity in the optic nerve. A code which transmits all of the input message is said to be reversible; that is, the information received at the output can be used to reconstruct completely the input message. The receptors do not seem to be constructed to provide a completely reversible code.

Many forms of energy change can be observed when a message is followed from the receptor organ to a nerve and thence to the cortex of the human brain. Conduction along the nerve fiber itself is a complicated electrical phenomenon, but it is not like an electric current in a wire. At the synapses, complicated chemical reactions occur which may produce permanent changes. A detailed account of the transmission of the message within the central nervous system cannot be given with the same clarity with which one can describe the transduction of telephone messages through sophisticated electronic amplification equipment. The reason is that there are technical difficulties involved in the exploration of biological transduction, and the tracing of impulses involves following them through minute and intricately interwoven structures which cannot be mapped out at this time. There is also the additional complication produced by the fact that the structures are, undoubtedly, not uniform within any one species. Also, a message may follow different paths on different occasions. What is known about the transduction process and the coding which it involves can be discussed at this time only in the most general terms.

The coding of information by the nervous system can be explored from two different approaches. On the one hand, the physiologist explores, for example, receptor activity and studies the relationship between information inputs and outputs of receptors, and by this means discovers what characteristics of inputs are coded by the receptor and transmitted as outputs. On the other hand, the psychologist attempts to discover what aspects of the information available to the organism can form the basis for learning, and from such data he can make inferences about the coding capacity of the receptor and nervous system. For example, psychological data make it clear that the nervous system has very limited capacity for coding information related to the location of sounds, but is well equipped for coding information related to pitch. Such psychological studies provide evidence concerning the capacity of various perceptual systems to transmit various kinds of information.

Physiological Data about Coding at the Receptor Level

While it is common knowledge that the impact of appropriate energy, force, or chemical solution to a receptor nerve results in the transmission of a nerve impulse along an *afferent fiber,* the process involves much more than a simple coding of the energy impinging on the receptor into a set of nerve impulses. Several other effects appear to be involved which have considerable consequence.

First, there is some evidence that the actual sensitivity of a receptor may be reduced or inhibited by central processes. That central neural processes can influence the transduction of information at the receptor level is a concept having important implications for all educational processes involving the transmission of information to human receivers. Consider, for example, the fact that stimulating a brain structure known as the *midbrain integumentum* induces a lasting augmentation of the frequency of firing of individual ganglion cells in the retina both in spontaneous firing and in response to a flash illumination. The importance of such a finding is that it opens up the possibility that blocking of information can occur at all levels of the nervous system down to the receptor level itself.

Second, the firing of one receptor may influence the rate of firing of other receptors within the same sensory system. To further illustrate this phenomenon, we may cite experiments reported in a study by Hartline and Ratliff (1956–57). The study undertook the simultaneous measurement of the frequency of the discharge of nerve impulses from two visual receptor units of a simple organism called limulus enabling the exact description of the interaction of the two receptors. The inhibition that is exerted mutually among the receptor units in the eye of limulus was analyzed by recording oscillographically the discharge of nerve impulses in each optic nerve fiber separately. Receptor units were illuminated independently by separate optical systems. The frequency of the maintained discharge of impulses from each of two receptors illuminated steadily is lower than when each is illuminated by itself. When only two receptors are illuminated, the magnitude of the inhibition of each one depends only on the degree of activity of the other. The activity of each, in turn, is the result of the direct excitation from light and the inhibition exerted on it by the other. The excitation of one receptor results in the inhibition of neighboring receptors. This is the process known as *lateral inhibition.* The general effect of this process is to emphasize boundaries of objects and lines in the visual scene that divide areas with strong brightness contrast. The over-all effect is to convert the picture of the world into something approaching a line drawing.

Third, it has been shown recently, using microelectrode techniques, that a part of all sensory transducers spontaneously fire, even when deprived of their usual stimulation. This can be shown by recording optic-nerve impulses from a single nerve fiber while an animal such as a cat is in complete darkness. The impulses recorded in this instance arise from instability of the receptor organs rather than from actual stimuli. Receptors fire at intervals, even when not exposed to external energy sources, and thus the response to external stimulation produces a neural discharge rate which is superimposed upon the base rate of firing. It appears that the nervous system keeps at least some of its receptor elements in readiness for firing and at such a sensitivity level that very small amounts of energy are sufficient to trigger impulses. In fact, the spontaneous firing may be a necessary and integral part of the input conditions involved in sensory perception, transduction, and transmission.

Fourth, mechanical analysis of data occurs in conjunction with the activity of many receptors. This fact is most obviously a matter of importance in the coding of auditory information. The inner ear makes a mechanical analysis of the particular frequencies involved in sound and transmits the information thus analyzed to the higher centers. The sound of a given pitch produces maximum activity at one particular point in the *basilar membrane,* the main resonating structure in the inner ear; it is also capable of producing lesser effects at other points. In this way, the pitch of a sound is mechanically analyzed and coded. This activity provides a system of space coding in which the specific location of a receptor in the basilar membrane determines the message it will transmit. Oddly enough, in the case of the ear, the intensity of the physical stimulus is not generally coded in terms of frequency of nerve impulse in the auditory nerve. In the case of the other senses, an increase in the intensity of the stimulus produces an increase in the frequency of impulses in the corresponding nerve.

While the relationship of the inputs of information to the basilar membrane and the coded output is extremely complex, there is one type of auditory input which bears a simple relationship to the output. When frequencies below 2,000 cycles per second impinge on the basilar membrane, volleys of impulses tend to be produced in the auditory nerve. These volleys are at the same frequency as the sound which produced them. Thus when music is played into the ear of the cat, the auditory nerve of the cat can be tapped and a crude version of the music can be picked up from the nerve and played back.

The complexity of the problem of coding at the receptor is well illustrated by some common phenomena related to the analysis of visual data. The bulk of the evidence indicates that the retina functions as though there were three distinct systems of receptors involving the analysis of color. The argument in favor of this position goes back to a demonstration provided by Thomas Young more than 150 years ago that all the colors of the spectrum could be produced by combining varying amounts of red light, green light, and light in the blue-violet range. For this reason, the three colors—red, green, and blue—became known as the *primary colors,* and the hypothesis was that the retina contained three sets of color-sensitive cells corresponding to the three primary colors. The color transparencies which the tourist produces with his camera are all based on the same concept, that combinations of the three primary colors will produce any color in the spectrum. However, Gregory (1966) points out that some colors we see every day cannot be produced by a simple combination of red, green, and blue light in appropriate amounts. Brown is one such color. If one has three beams of light of the three different primary colors and projects them onto the same place on a wall, and if one can vary the intensity of each, one can produce a great range of colors, but never brown. Nevertheless, a color transparency which also produces the various colors by combining varying amounts of light of the three primary colors does show us areas, such as the trunks of trees, that are unmistakably brown in color. The experience of the color brown seems to be dependent upon the complex arrangement of the three primary colors. Such complex arrangements, particularly when they involve familiar objects, result in the seeing of colors which one would not expect to be there in terms of what we know about the spectrum. What this means is that when colored lights are presented in a complex pattern, more colors are seen than when the lights are present in some simple arrangement. Color depends on the spectrum wavelengths of the lights present, on their arrangement, and on the extent to which they do or do not represent familiar objects.

Color analysis may begin at the level of the retina, but the complete perception of color in a complex presentation such as a color slide almost certainly involves information analysis at all levels of the nervous system. If color analysis were confined to the retina, one would never be able to see many hues, including brown. The perception of color is an extremely complex matter which is not going to be understood through a study of the eye alone. Color perception is part of a complex perceptual mechanism involving all levels of the nervous system.

The Dimensions of Coding Provided by the Sensory Systems

The discovery of the coding system of the receptors has importance for psychologists interested in the design of information-transmission systems. This problem has been of particular concern to psychologists engaged in the design of aircraft, for the pilot must be provided with a flow of information both with respect to the internal operation of the aircraft and with respect to such matters as location, altitude, course relative to other aircraft, and so forth. The information must be supplied in a form which is easily coded by the operator. That some forms of information are more readily coded than others is manifestly clear. For example, a person can easily determine whether a light is on the left or the right of the operator, but he cannot determine with comparable accuracy whether a sound comes from a point to the left or the right. It is well established that the nervous system has much greater capacity for coding information with respect to location of source in the case of vision than sound. Most of the available knowledge concerning the dimensions in terms of which messages can be coded is derived from the study of the auditory and visual systems, though in recent times interest has been shown in exploring touch. Since our concern here is mainly with vision and hearing, the discussion will be limited to these systems.

It is of interest to compare the processes of coding involved in audition and vision. There are six useful dimensions which provide some accuracy for coding in the case of vision: the two spatial coordinates, and intensity, wavelength, time, and depth. Auditory coding, for all practical purposes, involves only three dimensions of coding, namely, intensity, frequency, and time. A fourth dimension of the auditory, localization, is so inefficient that it is hardly worth adding as a means of transmitting information in a civilized culture, though it may have been the carrier of information with survival value in more primitive times. One would not, for example, ever replace a green-red warning-light system on an aircraft with a warning system in which a sound to the left of the operator means safety and a sound to the right means danger. The greater number of available dimensions for coding probably makes vision the preferred channel of communication in many situations. The mere number of available coding dimensions may not be the only factor operating in the preference commonly shown for visual presentations. Another factor may be that the whole technology for presenting visual information is much better developed and has had a longer history than the technology of auditory presentation, which had to await the electronic age for it to move much beyond the use of the human voice. Henneman and Long (1954) imply that much needs to be done to develop auditory techniques for transmitting information and that prejudice in favor of the visual may be to some extent the product of inadequate technology.

Learning may involve the ability to make either absolute judgments or relative judgments. Man is generally much better at making relative judgments, and many learning situations are designed to take advantage of this fact. An example of a relative judgment is that of deciding which of two men is the taller. On the other hand, if one had to judge the height in inches of a particular man, this would involve an absolute judgment. Relative judgments are more accurate than absolute judgments. Thus a medical book shows side-by-side illustrations of healthy and malignant cells, and a book for antiquarians shows pictures of both genuine antiques and fine reproductions of them.

Man's ability to make relative judgments has often been determined by finding out what is the smallest noticeable difference that he can identify. For example, individuals tested on their ability to discriminate tones that differ in pitch may be found to be just able to discriminate tones that differ by one-hundredth of an octave. This amount, one-hundredth of an octave, is referred to as a *just noticeable difference* (j.n.d.). The term indicates the ability of the individuals to make such judgments. If a task were being designed that involved judging which one of two tones is the higher, then it would be important to be sure that the differences involved were several times the size of the just noticeable difference. Thus the j.n.d. is a convenient measure of the sensitivity of individuals for recognizing particular differences.

While the conclusion may be drawn that in the case of vision most of the dimensions by which information is coded have been fully exploited, the hearing channel appears to have a much greater capacity for transmitting information than current communication techniques imply, and an advanced technology could well improve vastly the use of auditory dimensions for the transmission of information. For example, there is the possible improved use of auditory cues in learning many motor tasks. In learning to use a rifle, the marksman might well be warned by the sound of a tone that he was off target, and the amount off target could be indicated by the loudness of the tone or the pitch of the tone. Ordinary speeds of speech probably grossly underuse the coding capacity of the human ear, and yet little is known about the capacity of humans to learn to use much higher speeds of verbal information transmission. While coding dimensions place a limitation on what can be transmitted, the human speaker typically operates far below that limit.

In this section we have considered certain limits that are placed on the coding of information in terms of the capacity of the sensory systems to utilize information provided by the environment. This aspect of coding should not be confused with the coding involved in the use of language, a matter which will be discussed much more extensively in other parts of this book.

Control Exercised by the Higher Centers

All controls within the central nervous system are subservient to the control exercised by the cerebral hemispheres. These are the structures that perform information analysis at the highest levels of complexity, and most of the complex information that is stored is stored within the cerebral hemispheres.

The two cerebral hemispheres can be regarded in many ways as two separate brain systems. At least, there is sufficient duplication of function between them that extensive damage may occur to one without the individual's over-all ability to handle problems being seriously reduced. There are many exceptions to this statement as is evident from the fact that damage to Broca's area, on the left side of the brain, produces an inability to produce speech though the person may continue to understand what is said to him. In contrast, frontal lobotomy, which involves severing fibers in the frontal area, has almost no effect on the patient when it is performed on only one side, though the same operation performed on both sides may produce marked changes in behavior.

The brain probably has an entirely different system for storing information than do most of the information-storage systems developed by man. The typical system developed by man for storing information is based on the idea that each piece of information stored is to be found in a particular place. Libraries are built on this principle. A particular book in a library belongs in a specified place and in no other place. A piece of information given to a computer is placed in a particular storage location where it can always be located. Storage in the brain tissue does not appear to involve this kind of pigeonholing of information. Information in the brain appears to be stored in multiple locations, perhaps with the advantage of permitting a great diversity of information items to be associated together or related to one another. This kind of storage system is suggested by the fact that damage to areas of the cortex not having specific functions does not generally result in the loss of memory of specific items of information.

The Higher Centers as Information-Analysis Systems

In the matter of the transmission of sensory information to the higher centers of the brain, one has to keep from imagining that a picture of the outside world somehow arrives at the higher centers and is stored there as a picture. The difficulty of this kind of thinking is as follows. Consider the fact that an image of the outside world is impressed upon the retina. Now suppose that this image is transmitted in an intact form to the cortex of the brain. What happens to it there? Is there a little man in the cortex who then takes a look at this brain picture and interprets it? Does the little man have eyes with retinal images that are, in turn, transmitted to his cortex, where another little man . . . ? The argument is quite obviously so much nonsense. The adjustment of the organism to the environment involves the intake and utilization of information. This utilization of information requires that it involve some kind of analysis, and the crucial questions to answer are, What kind of analysis takes place, and how is it undertaken?

Some of the most interesting cues at the physiological level are found in the work of Hubel and Wiesel (1959), who were able to record cortical responses in the brain of the cat to various visual displays. Hubel (1963) has provided an excellent popular description of this work. The visual displays involved were lines of light displayed on a screen in front of the cat. Through the use of microelectrodes, these researchers were able to identify the condition under which particular cells in the visual area of the cortex became activated. What they found was that particular cells fired for lines at particular angles. A cell that would fire when a line was presented at one angle would not fire when the angle was changed. Also, the nearer a cell was to the surface of the brain the more likely it was to be fired by a very specific position of the line. It appeared that the layers of cells represented a series of analyzers, with those deep in the cortex responding to more general categories than those nearer the surface. These findings fit well the hypothesis that the analysis of visual information involves the analysis of particular attributes. Such a system could offer some economy in information analysis.

The detailed analysis of incoming data is not always the exclusive responsibility of the higher centers. For example, studies of the optic nerve of the frog by Lettvin and his associates (1959) indicate that, in such a creature, information analysis may take place at the retinal level and at the level of the optic nerve. What has been demonstrated is that four different kinds of fibers of the optic nerve of the frog seem to carry four different kinds of information about particular aspects of the environment. Some fibers may carry information about small shadows and, hence, would have the function of signifying the presence of flying insects in the animal's field of view. Other fibers carry information about the appearance of large, moving edges such as occur when the frog is approached by larger predators. Others provide information about local, sharp edges such as those made by some obstacle. Still others provide information about the curvature of objects. The point to note is that the selection of this information from the complex visual field of the frog requires a complex analysis system, and this the frog has in a part of the nervous system outside of the main brain structures. Most neurologists assume that, in higher organisms, similar information analyses take place in the main brain structures and not peripherally, but this is still a matter of conjecture.

The visual systems of lower organisms, such as the frog, suggest that these creatures may be endowed with certain visual-analysis mechanisms essential for their survival. The extent to which man is thus endowed is controversial. The adult who gains vision for the first time through a corneal graft perceives a world filled with separate and distinct things, though he cannot identify these things nor name their attributes. Such a person is aware of the fact that an experimenter is holding an object in front of him, but he cannot identify it as a square, he cannot recognize it as an object having corners, and he cannot count the sides or corners. However, he does recognize it as an object separate from the other objects in the world. His visual-analysis system can go that far, but extensive experience and learning are necessary before many of the specific features of objects can be identified. What is said here does not mean that the human is not endowed with any mechanisms for recognizing specific features in his visual field, for there is some evidence to show that he does have some endowment in this respect.

The Nervous System as a Sequential Analyzer

Since there is substantial evidence that the analysis of information occurs, to some degree, in a sequential procedure within the nervous system, there is considerable speculation about where the various steps in the analysis occur. Although the concept of sequential analysis is derived from experimental research, this concept of information analysis fits well our own daily experience. It is quite obvious that incoming information is exposed to some quite crude analysis at a level in the nervous system where we have little awareness. We may not be aware of the music played through the intercom until the piece suddenly comes to an end. The fact that we do note the end of the music indicates that our nervous system was registering the presence of music. It is also clear that the registration did not involve analysis of the incoming signals to the point where the piece of music was identified. One can perhaps consider the analysis of the incoming signals related to the music to be such that they can be analyzed at a number of levels. Perhaps the lowest level of analysis would be that in which the nervous system records that there is a sound source. At a more complex level the sound is identified as music. At a third level the piece of music is identified as being a particular piece. At the next level the music is identified in terms of the instruments involved. And at the most complex level, details concerning the musical quality of the performance are identified. When music forms just a vague background, as it does when it is played in a bank or supermarket, analysis is at the lower levels, but the person listening to a concert sets himself the task of undertaking the most complex analysis.

The same kind of sequential analysis occurs in the perception of visual objects. In the latter case, analysis may vary in complexity and detail from that in which an object is identified merely as something to be avoided during locomotion, up to the complex level where its characteristics are analyzed in terms of subtle details. At the most complex level, information is also often analyzed in terms of analogies. For example, a chemistry teacher can represent atoms by a picture of billiard balls with arms on them through which they become attached to other atoms. Now it is perfectly evident that atoms do not resemble billiard balls with hands projecting from them, but they do have a relation to the real phenomenon. At the complex levels of analysis, information is sometimes analyzed in terms of such relations. One can reasonably assume that analysis at this level must occur in the cortex. One can be much more sure of such a proposition than of any proposition suggesting that lower levels of analysis occur at lower levels of the nervous system.

Holding Mechanisms

The nervous system has to include devices for the temporary holding of information. Many sources of evidence indicate the necessity of such systems. An animal confronted with two upside-down pans and shown some food placed under one of the pans will manifest a continuing food-seeking response in relation to the pan. Presumably, the information about the location of the food is held in temporary storage. The sound of a bell can become associated with the presence of food, even though the sound of the bell and the presence of food are separated by several seconds' duration. Once again, one has to assume that the signal provided by the bell is held as information long enough for it to become tied to the inputs related to food. This temporary storage requires that the nervous system have what are called *temporary holding mechanisms*.

The reality of these holding mechanisms has been demonstrated in isolated pieces of living brain tissue in which an electrical stimulus can sometimes be shown to initiate activity that the nervous tissue can maintain over relatively long periods of time. Just how this activity is maintained within the nervous tissue is still a matter of conjecture, though our knowledge of nerve activity indicates that there are only a few possibilities. Activity cannot be maintained within a single cell for any length of time. An impulse that begins to pass down an axon moves along the length of the fiber, but expires if it does not initiate further activity at its termination. In the dendrites, an impulse may fade away as it moves toward the cell, but activity beyond a small fraction of a second does not seem possible in a single cell. In addition, once a nerve impulse has passed down a nerve fiber, a recovery time is necessary before a new impulse can follow the same course.

Holding mechanisms obviously have to involve more than a single fiber, for the experimental evidence clearly establishes that activity initiated in a single fiber will be maintained for only a very short time, generally not more than a small fraction of a second. One possibility suggested originally many years ago by Lorente de Nó and developed by Hebb (1966) is that the central nervous system can hold information through groups of nerve cells arranged in a circular pattern. A nerve impulse might keep moving around the circular arrangement. An impulse might also move around one circular pattern and, once it returned to the point where it started, still find that the next nerve cell had not yet come out of the recovery period (*latency period*), in which case the impulse might initiate activity in a related circular arrangement of cells. Such loops of nerve cells provide a plausible explanation of how nerve activity can be maintained once it has been initiated.[1] However, one cannot demonstrate directly that such arrangements do actually exist. Indeed, there would be no practical way of dissecting out loops of cells that might provide the structural basis of holding mechanisms, but one can demonstrate the continuation of activity in masses of cortical tissue, once such activity has been initiated.

Outputs from the Nervous System

Since this book is concerned with the way in which man handles inputs of information, one can very easily forget that these inputs involve much more than the activation of receptors, the coding of information, and the ultimate utilization of this information in the higher centers. The input would be very impoverished were it not for the fact that a muscular system exists which brings the receptors into a varying relationship with the environment. The eyes are not passive reception devices but means of *continuously scanning* the environment. This scanning can take place because relevant parts of the muscular system are being continuously activated through the *efferent* (or motor) *nerves*. Outputs from the nervous system to the muscles result in a continuous new input to the perceptual system. In this way the inputs of information are under continuous modification and provide a continuous flow of knowledge about the changing environment. An extraordinary fact about this muscular control of the information inputs is that the central nervous system is able to put

---

[1] Milner (1957) has pointed out that the difficulty of the Hebb proposal is that it represents a runaway system with no brakes. Milner elaborates the system to include inhibitory pathways.

together the information, picked up piecemeal, into a coherent and unified picture of the surrounding world.

The fact that muscular adjustments can vary the input to the perceptual systems is important in understanding certain aspects of problem solving. For example, if one is faced with the problem of discovering why an electric clock does not work, one may begin by directing one's gaze toward various aspects of the clock and its related equipment. One may, for example, move one's gaze along the cord and establish whether or not it is plugged in. One may place an ear against the clock and find out whether it is producing a characteristic hum. One may explore the interior of the clock after removing the case. All of these activities require a close cooperation between the receptor system and the muscles that orient the receptors toward particular aspects of the environment. Substantial learning is involved in the acquisition of skill related to the effective derivation of information from the environment.

There are also other ways in which the outputs of the motor nerves and muscular system may facilitate the taking in and organization of information. One may, for example, count observed events on one's fingers. One may obtain help in the visualization of an object by representing an object, in a rough way, with one's hands. In learning to tie a knot, by first observing a demonstration and then attempting to tie it oneself, the observation of the knot-tying alone may be a poor source of information that is not readily retained. However, when one attempts to tie the knot oneself, and ultimately succeeds, the information derived from the muscles appears to provide a source of information that is much more readily retained. Indeed, there is a great amount of evidence indicating that self-initiated activity provides information more readily retained than information that is received through the eye or the ear and involving only a minimum of muscular activity. The old adage that learning by doing is more effective than learning by observation has some truth to it, although the reason for it is still rather obscure.

At one time, psychologists believed that thinking necessarily involved outputs to the muscles, which in turn produced *kinesthetic sensations* (sensations of movement), which in turn stimulated further thought. Some thinking may take place by this kind of a mechanism, but evidence clearly shows that many thought processes are quite independent of the innervation of the muscles. This fact can be demonstrated through the use of curare, a drug that has the property of blocking the passage of nerve impulses from motor nerves to muscles. When curare is injected into a human, all of his skeletal muscles become completely relaxed. Breathing then has to be maintained artificially or death would result. The point of great interest in the present connection is that such a person who has lost all capability of using his muscles still is able to take in and retain information and to undertake some thinking. The demonstration shows that movement is not absolutely necessary for thought, although movement may sometimes facilitate thought.

Chapter 3

The Internal Analysis of Perceptual Information

The preceding chapters have presented the general nature of the perceptual systems and some of the characteristics of the nervous system as an information-processing device. These materials provide background for the following chapters, which have to do mainly with behavior related to information reception, processing, and storage.

Information is received by the sensory systems. It is then recognized or identified in some way. Beyond that point the information may be handled in a number of different ways. It may be almost immediately forgotten. It may be held in short-term storage, or it may be placed in permanent memory. Another possibility is that it may be used immediately for making a decision, before being discarded from the perceptual system. In this chapter, the main concern is with the problem of how information comes to be identified or recognized by the perceptual system.

Some Events in the Perceptual Process

Let us begin this discussion with some results produced by Sperling (1960) in a study of visual perception. Sperling presented for 50 milliseconds a display consisting of nine letters arranged in three rows of three letters each. Shortly after the display had been turned off, a tone was sounded which was either high, low, or medium in pitch. The subjects were given prior practice in identifying the pitch. The discrimination of the tones was an easy task. Each subject was instructed that immediately after the letters had been flashed on the screen, he was to speak the letters of the top row if the high tone had sounded, the middle row for the medium tone, and the bottom row for the low tone. Sperling showed that his subjects could do this very easily. This is hardly surprising, but what is surprising is that although the subjects could recall the designated row, they could not recall more than occasional letters from the other rows. Without the signal, subjects could recall four or five letters. Similar results were found by Averbach and Coriell (1961), who used an arrow to indi-

45

cate a particular letter that was to be recalled. The arrow appeared shortly after the letters were turned off.

What is important here is the interpretation of the results. Since the signal tone came after the letters had been presented and after they had been turned off, the subjects in the experiment were not reading the letters from the display. They must have been reading them from some internal trace of the display that lasted longer than the letters. However, this trace did not last indefinitely, for if the signal were delayed for about 2 seconds, then the subjects were not able to recall the row correctly. One must assume that the internal trace left by the display of letters faded within this 2-second interval. This leads one to suppose that the viewing of any display for a brief interval leaves behind a short-lived trace of the display from which information can be read, much in the same way that information can be read from the original display. The data suggest also that only a limited amount of information can be read from the trace, perhaps because the trace fades before all of it can be used. The trace represents a very temporary storage system capable of holding information for only a few seconds.

Some writers interpret these findings as indicating that all the visual information enters a *preperceptual field* and that the letters designated as those to be recalled are moved from the preperceptual field into the *perceptual field* where they then become available for further examination, reading out, or even memorization. All of the nine letters cannot enter the perceptual field at once, since the perceptual field is a limited-capacity system; the tone designates the letters that are to be thus transferred to this limited-capacity system. All the information provided by the retina is, presumably, placed in the preperceptual field where it has a short life and fades within perhaps two or three seconds. The phenomenon is highly reminiscent of that described by Hull in his later work (1951), in which he proposed that a *stimulus trace* persisted for a few seconds after the stimulus had been removed. Hull introduced the concept of stimulus trace in order to explain how the unconditioned stimulus came to be hooked up with the conditioned response. The Hull construct of stimulus trace is closely similar to that of a preperceptual field, the main difference being that the former has a physiological flavor while the latter savors more of personal experience.

In addition, some of the information in the stimulus trace or preperceptual field is selected and retained in a less transient memory system for further utilization. The information that is thus selected represents, in our present terminology, the *perceptual field*. The reader should note that both terms of central importance, the *preperceptual field* and the *perceptual field,* are constructs and do not denote aspects of personal experience.

The constructs we have been considering carry with them certain important implications. One is that the preperceptual field or stimulus trace represents a high-capacity information system, with about the same information capacity as that of the retina and optic nerve. If the entire stimulus trace is a record of the crude data involved in the perceptual system, then it has to represent a high-capacity system. A second implication is that the trace lasts long enough for certain components to be retained for further examination—a fact which clearly indicates that the perceptual field, as defined here, is a system of far more limited capacity than the preperceptual field. In other words, there is a selection of data at a very early stage in the perceptual process, and this selection results in a substantial reduction in the amount of information with which the person has to deal.

The transitory traces of information lasting a few seconds that have been discussed here have been described by Broadbent (1958) as representing a *short-term memory*. We will not use this term in reference to these phenomena because it has come to be applied mainly to retention phenomena of longer duration. The current usage is to discuss the kind of retention found in, for example, most verbal-learning experiments as representing a short-term memory phenomenon.

The distinction between a stimulus trace and information in short-term memory, like most distinctions in this area, is not as clear as one would like. Consider, for example, the case of a rather transitory trace, discussed by Broadbent (1958), in which a person looks up a telephone number and remembers it just long enough to dial it. Broadbent points out that although one may remember such a number for only a few seconds, the memory of the number for longer periods can be facilitated by repeating it to oneself just before the original trace faded. In this way, one can look up a number, walk over to the telephone while repeating the number to oneself, and then dial the number. If the number is not put back into the trace system by repeating it to oneself, it is quickly forgotten; but even if it has been repeated a few times, while walking across the room, it rapidly fades after the last repetition. This phenomenon is much more like a memory trace, in that it involves information retained for only a few seconds, and yet it involves the kind of repetitive process typically found in studies of short-term memory with nonsense syllables. One may well ask, What kind of trace is involved when a number is repeated to oneself? On the surface it is not the kind of stimulus trace that occurs when one listens to a message or views a visual display, particularly if the repetition under one's breath is too faint to be auditory. There is the possibility that the kinesthetic sensations from the vocal mechanism might be the basis of a trace. The characteristics of the stimulus trace and the short-term memory mechanism are not sufficiently well understood to make a clear differentiation at this time.

Again, it must also be made clear that there is also no clear-cut distinction between short-term memory, as the term is used in laboratory verbal-learning studies, and permanent memory. The distinction disappears when one recognizes that typical verbal-learning procedures have been shown to leave marks that can influence behavior as much as a week later, even though the subjects in the study had no knowledge that the information was to be used later; see, for example, Judson, Cofer, and Gelfand (1956). Indeed, what really determines whether information will or will not be deposited in a system of permanent storage remains obscure.

The phenomenon of a stimulus trace is not peculiar to the visual system alone, but is probably shared by all of the perceptual systems. The understanding of a spoken word requires that the sound of the early part of the word be held as a trace long enough so that the whole word can be perceived. In the hearing of a word such as "window," it is quite evident that the first part of the word, "win," has to be retained until "dow" has been heard. Otherwise, the word could not be perceived and comprehended. The evidence suggests that the stimulus trace for auditory inputs has a duration about as long as that for visual inputs, or perhaps a little less. While these phenomena are referred to here as stimulus traces, Neisser (1967) proposes alternative terminology. In the case of the transitory record of visual events, he uses the term *iconic memory*. The corresponding phenomena in the auditory area he refers to as *echoic memory*. The trace system represents a basic holding mechanism which permits us to scan a complex set of information and take from it the component elements needed. There is little knowledge available about what kind of neurological mechanism is involved.

Finally, it seems clear that we have some capacity for clearing out stimulus traces from our perceptual system. When one rapidly glances around a room one has just entered, each glance in a new direction initiates a new stimulus trace. In such glancing around, the various stimulus traces initiated do not seem to produce perceptual confusion. Either one is able to ignore the old stimulus traces as one turns one's attention to some new set of objects, or the perception of the new set of objects eradicates all previous stimulus traces. Again, reading is performed by fixating groups of words for very short intervals of time, and the perception of each group of words is not disrupted by the stimulus traces of the words fixated just a fraction of a second earlier. Those who have *eidetic images,* commonly referred to as "photographic memories," sometimes show an interference between what they have just attended to and what they are now attending to, perhaps because they have difficulty in getting rid of or erasing stimulus traces.

Figure and Ground

The distinction between a preperceptual field and a perceptual field is closely similar to the distinction made by the gestalt psychologists between figure and ground. The latter distinction is not so much inferred from experimental data as it is from our daily experience that we perceive some part of our environment as having objectlike properties and that this part of our environment is perceived as a figure against a background in which little detail has been differentiated. For example, when we attend to one face in a crowd, the other faces melt into a background of which we are dimly aware. We still know there are other faces there, but the details escape us. The fact to which we attend is the *figure;* the other faces are the *ground.* Such a differentiation can be inferred to occur early in life. The fact that a baby will fixate, and follow, a bright light has been commonly cited as evidence that he is making this kind of differentiation.

The figure-ground differentiation, within the present context, reflects the fact that the perceptual system is a limited-capacity system and selects certain aspects of the inputs of information for a more detailed analysis than that to which the entire array of inputs can be exposed. Although the *figure* is exposed to a detailed analysis (that is, its features are clearly recognized), the *ground* is not ignored but is analyzed only at a relatively crude level. The crude analysis of the ground would seem to be necessary in order for that aspect which is to become the figure to be identified.

The process of attention has several components, but one of these is the identification of one part of the perceptual input as ground. The conditions which result in one part of the input becoming differentiated as figure, rather than another, will be considered in greater detail in those later sections that deal with the matter of attention.

Recognition Processes

The previous discussion has implied throughout that incoming information is to some degree identified or classified. A mass of faces in a crowd is identified as a mass of faces and not as a mass of watermelons, even though the individual faces are not recognized. A particular face that one recognizes in a crowd is identified as that of a particular person, and this identification involves a more precise level of analysis. Nevertheless, the recognition of a face as that of a particular person does not mean that all of the details of the face are seen. One can recognize a friend without ever knowing the color of his eyes or the shape of his nose. The recognition of his face involves a more precise analysis of the information than does the mere recognition of it as a face, but it does not involve the ultimate in detailed analysis. The problem to which we now turn is how recognition takes place, that is, how the perceptual systems identify particular batches of incoming information for what they are.

Recognition of both the visual and the auditory material is probably a prerequisite for learning and for more complex thinking processes to occur. What the process of recognition involves and the conditions under which it can be facilitated are, therefore, matters of great interest to those concerned with the audiovisual field. The rate at which recognition takes place is also a matter of considerable interest.

Three main theories have been developed to account for recognition in any of the perceptual systems. The reader who is interested in knowing more about these theories is referred to Neisser (1967). The discussion presented here will provide a brief review of current thought on the matter. The first and oldest of these is what has been termed *template matching*. According to this theory of recognition, the visual presentation of an object or pattern such as a square takes place through the perceived square being matched with a stored representation of a square. This theory of recognition makes the assumption that what is stored in memory is a set of representations of objects and phenomena. Recognition involves the matching of the perceived object with the stored representation of the object. This is the theory of recognition in its crudest form, but to make it work at all, considerable additional complexities have to be introduced into it. First, some acknowledgment has to be made of the fact that no serious student of memory takes the position that the human storage is filled with records of specific experiences. Long ago, Head (1920) proposed a theory, later popularized by Bartlett (1932), that memory traces represent consolidated traces of numerous past experiences. These consolidated traces were referred to as *schemata*. Thus, one's memory of an oak tree would not represent a series of memories of particular oak trees, but would be represented by a single representation that incorporated the common features of all oaks that had been observed. In such a case, an oak tree that one had not previously seen or identified would be matched with the stored schema. If the match was a good one, then the tree would be identified as an oak. If the match was a poor one, then the object involved would be rejected as an oak, but perhaps then might be matched with schemata derived from experiences with other trees, such as beech, or elm, or maple.

Scientists have generally responded rather negatively to the template theory of recognition. The arguments against such a theory are not particularly conclusive, and seem to stem largely from the scientist's position that if he were to develop a system for recognizing patterns, he would not use a template system at all. The objections center around the fact that a particular object, such as a cup, is recognized regardless of whether it is large or small, whether it is upside down or right side up, or even whether it has any one of a wide variety of shapes. It is very difficult to imagine a schema or template of a cup which would provide a reasonable match for all of the varied cups that could be correctly matched with it. One way out of this difficulty is to assume that there is not just a single template of a cup, but several. If the object presented matches any one of these, then it is classified as a cup. Then one is left with the question of how many templates there are; perhaps there are as many templates as cups previously encountered. The latter position ceases to be plausible since memory would then have to contain vast numbers of different templates. Most theories of memory assume that there is some consolidation of previous experience into categories, for there is presumed to be a certain economy in the internal storage system.

A second approach to the identification of form involves what is termed *attribute analysis* or *feature analysis*. The approach was first put forward in a symposium on *The Mechanization of Thought Processes* in two independent papers, one by Sutherland (1959) and the other by Selfridge (1959), the former a psychologist and the latter an engineer. Both articles have something of an engineering flavor about them and suggest that if the maker of man had been an engineer, this is the way in which he would have arranged the mechanics of his brain to permit him to recognize objects. The general underlying concept of this approach is that perception involves the identification of the features of the sensory input and that an object is identified from an inventory of the features. This kind of system would require, presumably, a rather limited number of features that were identified and, hence, a limited number of analyzers, each one of which would identify the presence or absence of a particular kind of component of the perceptual world. Just what the component attributes would be is far from clear in any form of this theory, and how the analyzers would function is also quite obscure. In a way, these feature analyzers could be thought of as miniature templates, each of which is capable of identifying one feature. They are very much like the kind of structures that Hebb (1966) postulates when he thinks of a small, resonant neural circuit that resonates in the presence of one particular perceptual component, such as a straight line, a component sound of speech, or whatever the basic elements of perception actually are. Just how a particular shape or speech phoneme could result in the resonance of a particular group of nerve cells in the brain is not generally explained by such theories, and there is no knowledge from neurology that could account for this. There is considerable evidence to support the position that recognition involves the identification of particular features of the input. In learning to read by a word-recognition method, children learn to identify words through such attributes as the particular length of the word, the first letter of the word, the location of double letters, and sometimes the location of the word in a sentence. Certainly, when the adult reads, he does not recognize words through an analysis of each word, letter by letter. The adult probably reads in much larger units, perhaps several words in length, and the attributes in these units make it possible to identify them as units.

The theory that perceptual recognition takes place through an analysis of the presence or absence of certain features or components also remains attractive to scientists for a very different reason from those already considered. The scientific popularity of the model stems from the fact that scientists have been able to develop devices for the recognition of patterns on the basis of this theory. There are many very important problems related to the matter of pattern recognition that have made this problem an extremely important one to attack. For example, if a device could be developed for recognizing handwritten addresses, many of the problems involved in the sorting of mail would be solved.

Much of the work on pattern recognition by mechanical, optical, and electrical systems has focused on the recognition of the letters of the alphabet. Some of the attempts have been to develop ways of recognizing handwriting. Studies on printed material have generally come closer to solving the problems involved than have those on handwriting. The reason is that in printed material each letter is separated by a space. The pattern analyzer then selects as the unit for analysis the figure that appears between spaces, that is to say, a letter. In handwriting, on the other hand, letters are usually not cut off from other letters, and the analytic devices have difficulty in determining what are the basic units to be analyzed. At the perceptual level, analysis seems to require that some phenomenon acquires figural properties that distinguish it from the background before identification seems to take place.

Methods for the recognition of printed letters generally involve several stages. For example, the letters of the alphabet can be divided into two groups: those that have closed loops (A, B, D, O, P, Q, and R), and those that do not. If the particular letter to be recognized is O, then the application of the criterion of the presence or absence of a closed loop narrows the recognition problem down to one of the seven closed-loop characters. A second characteristic to be analyzed might be that of determining whether or not the letter has a vertical line in it. If it did, then this would exclude the letters B, D, P, and R, leaving A, O, and Q. A third analyzer might then remove those that had more than one component, leaving the letter O as the letter identified. In the case of the human attempting to recognize letters, such analyzers could work either simultaneously or in a sequence one after the other. The evidence suggests that the analyzers operate simultaneously rather than in a multistage system. The latter assumption is necessary to account for the great speed with which recognition takes place. Also, it is clear that it takes no longer to recognize a two-digit number than a single digit. This would not be so if the analysis of the second digit could not take place until the analysis of the first digit had been completed. In the case of the two-digit number, the analysis of both digits must take place at the same time; otherwise, the time taken to recognize two digits would be twice that involved in the recognition of one digit.

A number of investigators, including Selfridge (1959) and Feigenbaum and Simon (1963), have. developed models involving the multistage analysis of materials. However, the multistage system is introduced in order to afford economy in the mechanisms involved and may not represent the system used by the nervous system. Some writers, such as Hebb (1966), prefer to imagine a system of analysis that involves a single stage. This would be a much less economic system of analysis in terms of the amount of analytical machinery needed in the nervous system, but the body is not necessarily built on the basis of engineering principles of efficiency.

At the present time, psychologists, psychoacoustic specialists, and others who have studied this problem are inclined to accept the theory that information analysis takes place in the perceptual system through the simultaneous operation of a very large number of different analyzers. These are presumed to work in parallel at the same time, and each is built to identify a particular feature of the perceptual input. The analyzers are presumed to operate completely automatically and are not considered to be under the executive control of the individual. Nobody has any idea about how many such analyzer mechanisms would have to exist in man in order to account for the very large number of different objects that man can recognize. However, a task such as letter recognition may not involve a very large number of different analyzers, provided a uniform style of print is used.

Some support for the attribute-analysis theory comes from studies of the development of young children. In learning to read, children identify words, not by identifying the total over-all form of the word, but by identifying specific features. A word may be identified because of the presence of particular letters or because it is a certain length or even because of its position in a sentence. The children show that they recognize words by recognizing specific characteristics and not gross characteristics.

Some evidence to support the theory that recognition is undertaken through a system of analyzers comes from comparative physiology and psychology. The work of Hubel and Wiesel (1959) shows that, in the case of the brain of the cat, visual information tends to be analyzed in terms of horizontal lines, vertical lines, and oblique lines. Different layers in the occipital lobes of the brain of the cat respond separately to each one of these categories of lines. What this finding tells us is that the cat has machinery for identifying the extent to which the input to the eye is structured in terms of horizontal, vertical, or oblique lines; but how the information thus analyzed is utilized to provide recognition is obscure. The evidence supports the theory of the existence of systems of information analyzers that identify particular attributes of the visual information, but that is all.

Work on the eye and the visual-analysis system in the nervous system of the frog by Lettvin and his associates (1959), discussed in the previous chapter, shows that the apparatus has the capacity for responding to certain buglike objects in the environment, but not to large, moving boundaries. Such evidence is, on the surface, very convincing support for a system of feature analyzers, perhaps even in man, until one recognizes that lower organisms *may* be built to recognize much more specific aspects of the environment than is man. Lower organisms tend to show specificity of function within the nervous system not found in man, who has large areas uncommitted to any identifiable specific function. The feature-analysis systems found in the frog and the cat may be peculiar to their particular stage of evolutionary development.

The first two theories of recognition discussed were developed largely in the context of visual tasks and the physiology of vision. The third type of model of recognition has emerged largely through research on speech, and it has been mainly a speech-recognition model. Indeed, interest in the model has come mainly from those interested in speech, though a few psychologists, for example, Neisser (1967), have viewed this third model as a good description of the visual-recognition mechanism also. The third model is referred to as the *analysis-by-synthesis model*. The essential concept underlying this model is most readily understood in a speech context. Suppose a person hears the spoken word "cat." The sound of the word enters the ear, where it is transferred, in some form, to a temporary holding mechanism in the brain. The theory postulates that the brain then makes successive attempts to build a word that has the same characteristics as the word "cat." When the brain succeeds in synthesizing a word that has a close match, then the brain knows that the word presented has the same meaning as the one synthesized. Presumably, it is possible for the brain to recognize the meaning of a word it has synthesized, but not to recognize directly a word presented. There are two distinct and separate theories about how words are synthesized. One involves what is known as the *Haskins model,* developed by Liberman (1957) at the Haskins Laboratories. It is called a *motor theory of speech perception,* in that the person synthesizes a word by moving the various muscles that produce speech. It is as if the person attempted to synthesize the speech he was hearing by talking to himself silently under his breath. This theory of analysis-by-synthesis is a little unlikely in view of the fact that speech recognition is very rapid and that muscle movements are quite slow.

The second theory of understanding speech by an analysis-by-synthesis process is more promising. It is known as the *Halle-Stevens model,* and like many models in this field of research, was developed by engineers. In this model, something resembling the speech that is heard is synthesized inside the nervous system, but does not involve silent speech. Halle and Stevens (1962) are quite specific about how the nervous system might make this comparison between speech coming in and speech synthesized. Presumably, talking in psychological terms, a comparison would be made between the perceived speech and the image of the speech synthesized, but those who have proposed the theory do not go as far as to say this. Indeed, the Halle-Stevens theory is presented in the original article in quite precise engineering terms.

Neisser is able to bring forward fairly convincing arguments to support the analysis-by-synthesis position. He is impressed with the fact that in many situations people perceive what is *not* there. In reading a book, one is likely to read a word as correctly spelled even though the printer has misspelled it. Such errors are obvious after they have been pointed out. We see a person we expect to see on the street corner and are surprised when the person turns out to be a stranger. Neisser is particularly impressed with hallucinations, in which a person sees vividly objects that are not there. Since the hallucinations come from somewhere, Neisser hypothesizes that the person constructs them by a process which he terms *figural synthesis.* His position is that perception and imagination are parts of the same process. When the process is used to interpret the environment, one refers to *perception;* but when it is used to construct representations of objects not present, then the term *imagination* is applied. The concept that Neisser develops in this connection reflects great ingenuity.

Another very persuasive source of evidence comes from studies of what is known as the *verbal-transformation effect* (see Warren, 1968). This effect can be readily demonstrated with simple equipment. One method is to play on a tape recorder a small loop of tape which has had a single word recorded on it, so that the same word is played again and again as the loop passes over the recorder's head. The listener who hears the word played repeatedly reports changes in what he hears. For example, in one study, the word "tress" was recorded and played to a subject who reported frequent and dramatic changes in what he heard during a 3-minute period. This same subject reported hearing the words "stress," "dress," "Jewish," "Joyce," "florist," and "purse." These words represent an internal production of language. The phenomenon fits well into the theory that speech is recognized by an internal synthesis of whatever is heard. However, other explanations are also possible. The possibility must also be kept in mind that what happens in the transformation effect is an oddity, and not at all typical of what happens when ordinary speech is heard.

Those who endorse the analysis-by-synthesis theory find indirect support from work that has been undertaken on the recognition of handwritten words through mechanical and electrical devices. The major difficulty in this recognition task is that the letters are not separated by spaces in cursive writing and, hence, there is not a set of separate and distinct units presented for perceptual analysis. Faced with such a recognition task, the analyzer generates combinations of letters that make words and finds the combination that best fits the particular word being scanned. The important point to note is that the machine attempts to synthesize a word and match it to the word presented; it does not take the word as presented and analyze cues that permit the identification of the word. Although the analysis-by-synthesis position can be neither rejected nor accepted outright at this time, some comments need to be made here to indicate some of the problems that this system is likely to encounter.

First, it is dangerous to generalize from rare and unusual phenomena such as hallucinations and to conclude that perception involves a similar kind of process. It is going to be extremely difficult to demonstrate that the processes are similar. Also, the study of how engineers go about developing equipment that will read handwriting may not provide a good model of how the nervous system performs similar tasks. The nervous system does not conform to the usual principles of engineering design. The fact that engineers build machines that recognize handwriting by a process of analysis-by-synthesis is not a very convincing argument that the human uses the same procedure when confronted with the same kind of task.

Second, a major difficulty encountered, and implictly recognized by Neisser, is that analysis-by-synthesis might be expected to be quite a time-consuming operation and probably more time-consuming than template matching or feature analysis, since it involves a process of finding successively better and better approximations to the content of the visual trace. Since some forms of recognition take place with extreme rapidity, analysis-by-synthesis would appear to be out of the question in those tasks. For example, scanning tasks can be undertaken at a speed which virtually excludes an analysis-by-synthesis theory of perception. Workers in newspaper-cutting agencies, who scan newspapers for items pertaining to the interests of their clients, often scan printed material at the rate of 1,000 words per minute, and the search can be undertaken simultaneously for 100 or more items about which information is sought. Neisser tries to overcome this difficulty by suggesting that scanning tasks are, perhaps, different from most other tasks involving perceptual recognition. Neisser takes the position that scanning and searching tasks do not involve synthesis but depend on what he calls *preattentive control*. He proposes that there are preattentive recognition systems which permit a person to pick up the presence of certain cues or configurations in the sensory inputs. He is essentially arguing that the task of looking for something, when one knows exactly what one is looking for, is different in a highly practiced person from the task of being confronted with something and having to recognize it. Since the efficient performance of scanning tasks requires extensive practice, there is the possibility that the effect of practice may be to set up a special mechanism, but the argument is not particularly convincing.

Particularly damaging to the Haskins analysis-by-synthesis motor theory of speech perception is that at such institutions as the United Nations, interpreters will listen to and understand one language while they speak a translation of the message in another language. Since the vocal cords of the interpreters are fully occupied in speaking the translation, they cannot be used to produce a synthesis of the language that is being listened to and understood. In the face of such a difficulty, one probably has to abandon the theory that speech is recognized through synthesizing with the vocal cords a silent version of what is heard. Speech may be recognized by synthesis, but if so, it is synthesized without involving the vocal apparatus.

Although we have rejected the analysis-by-synthesis model of perception as a general model governing all recognition processes, there are occasions when perception may involve an internal synthesis. Familiar misperceptions—such as that of being sure that the figure across the street is a familiar friend when it is, in fact, a total stranger, who has a few points of resemblance to the friend—may well involve perception through internal synthesis. There are some rather puzzling laboratory demonstrations which give weight to the synthesis aspect of perception, such as the verbal-transformation effect. For example, an ink blot may be seen as a map or a butterfly or a biological preparation, demonstrating the role of synthesis in perception. There can be no question that synthesis plays a role in perception and that sometimes recognition may take place through an analysis-by-synthesis, but the weight of the evidence is that recognition generally takes place through a feature-analysis procedure.

The evidence discussed in connection with the recognition process indicates that perceptual analysis takes place through the simultaneous operation of large numbers of independent and specialized information analyzers. At least, the evidence points in this direction in the case of visual-information analysis. There is also some evidence touched upon earlier that auditory information, too, is analyzed by chunks. The auditory system is constructed in such a way that information from the receptor system has to be transmitted through a system that takes in information in a continuous flow. However, this does not mean that all analysis of auditory material is handled in a completely sequential manner. The system would be very uneconomical if it performed all analyses in the latter way. If each basic sound unit, that is, each phoneme, were to be identified separately in listening to speech, only a very inefficient analysis would result. This fact also becomes evident when one reflects on the fact that most of the phonemes involved in the enunciation of a single word have to be received before the word can be identified. It is necessary for the nervous system to delay analysis until the entire word has been received. In some cases, it would be even more economical for several words to be received before the analysis began. There is some evidence from paired-associate learning that this kind of delay in the analysis of meaning occurs. Suppose, for example, that subjects are learning to associate two words together. The first word presented is "chest." Now just what meaning to attribute to this word depends largely on the nature of the second word. If the second word is "jewelry," the first word will be given one meaning; but if the second word is "tuberculosis," the word "chest" will be given an entirely different meaning. Mueller and Travers (1965) have shown that efficient paired-associate learning occurs when both words to be associated are presented as quickly as possible, since the hookup of the two words cannot begin until both words have been received. Much the same probably happens in the everyday perception of language. Some of the incoming information is held in temporary storage until a sufficient quantity has been received to make analysis an effective and efficient operation.

Thus, the auditory system shows an information-processing system that is both sequential and simultaneous. Sounds go into the system in a sequence; then, when a chunk of a certain size has arrived and is retained in a temporary holding mechanism, the various parts of the chunk are simultaneously analyzed. The visual system, on the other hand, takes in large quantities of information simultaneously and then applies analysis to some limited aspect of the entire batch of information. Although we have some idea of the size of the batches of visual information processed at one time, we do not know whether the auditory system handles one word at a time, or several words, or short phrases.

Simultaneous and Successive Inputs

The point has been made that information handling, up to the point of recognition, involves both simultaneous and successive processes. Information analyzers appear to operate simultaneously, but the effective interaction with the environment requires that the information system handle a sequence of inputs. A related question is the extent to which two or more perceptual systems can function at the same time as analyzers of information. This question will be answered more fully in the next chapter in connection with the utilization of information; we are concerned here only with recognition rather than utilization.

When one is completely absorbed in a book, one may be quite unaware that the radio is playing in the next room or that there are children's voices in the street. One cannot generalize from this fact and take the position that the preoccupation with the book blocks all other information through all the other perceptual systems, or that no information analysis in relation to these other inputs is taking place. An important point to note is that certain information through other perceptual systems is immediately identified, as is evident from the fact that the calling of the reader's name produces an immediate response as does the call of "Fire" or "Help." In order for a person reading a book to respond to such signals through the auditory perceptual system while he is preoccupied with visual information, the incoming auditory information has to be analyzed at least at some crude level. One must presume that even when a person is completely occupied in taking in information through, say, vision, the information arriving through the other systems must be monitored, that is, analyzed and identified at a crude level so that crucial signals can be picked up and permitted to enter the perceptual field.

It is clear, then, that information can be monitored simultaneously by more than one of the perceptual systems—perhaps by all of the perceptual systems at the same time. This low-level monitoring of information through several systems represents the lowest level of cognitive activity.

Native Endowment of Perceptual Mechanisms

A problem of central importance to our understanding of perception is the extent to which the individual is natively endowed with the ability to analyze and organize sensory inputs. In reviewing the history of psychology over the past fifty years, one notes periods when great emphasis was placed on the supposed innate basis of perception, followed by periods when learning was viewed as the key. In the early part of the century, learning was emphasized as the basis of perception; but then came the gestalt psychologists, who took the position that the human was natively endowed to perform certain perceptual functions. One of these was to structure the sensory inputs so that some part of the input was perceived as a figure standing out against a vague and undifferentiated ground. What was differentiated in this way depended upon such features as intensity (the baby fixates a bright light) and form (the baby fixates a form such as a circular object presented against a uniform background). The laws of perception were considered to be largely matters of how the living organism was constructed to behave. An attempt was even made to suggest an innate physiological basis for the laws of perception. The arguments presented by the gestalt psychologists to support their position were attractive and persuasive, but the little evidence on which the arguments were based was derived largely from study of the adult, who is not a suitable subject if the problem is that of investigating the native aspects of perception.

Extremely damaging to the position of the gestalt psychologists concerning the innate basis of the perception of figure-ground relationships and form was the work of Hebb. In his classic work, *The Organization of Behavior* (1949), Hebb presented a substantial array of convincing pieces of evidence suggesting that not all of the perceptual behavior that gestalt psychologists had assumed to be independent of experience or "primitive" was actually that way. Hebb did accept the idea that the ability to structure figures and to contrast them with the ground was primitive and required no learning. He noted in this connection that Von Senden's patients (1932), who had been blind from birth and who gained vision for the first time through a corneal graft, did apparently perceive objects in the visual world even though they could not identify either the objects or the characteristics of the objects. They could not, for example, identify a square object as a square object, but they could say that there was an object in front of them with definite boundaries.

Hebb then went on to make the point that the gestalt psychologists had gone too far in proposing that the perceptual contrast of figure and ground was innate and, in addition, that the perception of form itself was innate. Hebb went on to introduce the concept of *object identity* in developing further ideas in this area. An object, as perceived, has identity, if its similarities and differences relative to other objects can be recognized. A person can show that a square and a triangle has for him identity if he can sort a mixed group of squares and triangles into the two separate categories. This the person blind from birth who gains sight cannot do at first. Such a person can note the fact that there are objects, but he cannot identify the attributes of the objects that give them identity.

Thus Hebb proposed that there are two fundamental aspects of perception: *unity,* which is innate and results in the object being recognized as a vague and amorphous something; and *identity,* which is learned. Identity permits the object to be recognized as one belonging to a particular class of object.

The perception of simple forms, in the sense that the forms are recognized as belonging to a group such as that designated as triangles or circles or squares, very clearly requires experience and is not, as the gestalt psychologists suggested, one of the givens of experience. It is learned. At least, all the evidence points in this direction. Hebb, in stressing this point, makes much use of the data provided by Von Senden and the behavior of his patients after they had recovered from the corneal-graft operation and had achieved sight for the first time. These patients generally shared one characteristic in common, namely, that only through prolonged training could they come to identify simple figures. One patient was able to distinguish between a square and a triangle only after weeks of training, but he could do so, even then, only by counting the corners. The kind of immediate recognition of a square as a square, and a triangle as a triangle, commonly taken for granted, simply did not take place until a more advanced stage of learning had been undertaken. Learning such simple identities as are involved in the perception of a square or a triangle appears to involve the learning of even simpler identities. For example, the learning of the identity of a triangle may first involve the learning of the identity of a corner or angle, such as is involved in a triangle. If this is so, then the learning of the identity of a triangle has to be preceded by the learning of the identity of an angle, consisting of two lines that meet at a point. In addition, acute and right angles may also have to be learned as having special identities.

What the basic elements in perceptual learning are is certainly not clear at this time, and they may well be culturally bound. For example, in the case of speech, the learning of the identity of particular speech components may be a necessary prerequisite for the comprehension of speech, but the fundamental phonemes differ from one language to another. Certain sounds that occur in one spoken language may simply not appear in another. Insofar as the identity of phonemes is a necessary precursor of the understanding of spoken language, one might expect that the basic perceptual learning may be different in different cultures. There is even some evidence that basic visual-perceptual components may also differ from one environment to another. The elemental identities that are learned involve, presumably, the establishment of what we called earlier in this chapter the basic analyzers, through whose activities objects are recognized.

Hebb's interesting analysis does not entirely settle the issue of what is learned and what is not learned in the perceptual process. A number of other research studies suggest that there may be other unlearned perceptual abilities in addition to those which have been considered. Hebb does point out that displays of color provide experiences which are givens in experience. Von Senden's patients enjoyed being exposed to colors from the start of their visual experience, and learned to name them relatively easily. In addition, there is some evidence that perception of distance has an inborn basis in man. A long series of studies have shown (see Walk & Gibson, 1961) that young animals of ten different species, ranging from turtles to humans, will avoid falling off edges where there is a vertical drop. When infants are placed on a flat surface and are coaxed to approach the experimenter who is on the other side of a sudden drop in the surface (covered with plexiglass in order to protect the infant from actually falling), the infant will not proceed over the cliff but will stop at the place where it begins. These infants can hardly have had the experience of falling from heights with punishing consequences, so that the drop in the floor level must somehow arouse inhibitions. Such an innate mechanism would have considerable survival value even in a civilized society in which the young are given some protection against such hazards.

A somewhat related phenomenon is reported by Bower (1966) on size constancy in very young infants. First let us consider what is meant by *size constancy*. Look at a man 20 feet away from you across the room; he will appear no smaller than a man only 10 feet away from you. Yet the image on the retina of your eye of the man 20 feet away is only half the linear size of the image of the man 10 feet away. Size constancy occurs because the interpretation of our perceptions takes into account the distance factor. The assumption has generally been made that a person is able to take into account distance as a factor in the interpretation of what he sees, because he has had experience of seeing the same object both near and far to him and knows that the object does not change merely because it is moved in relation to him. In this way, it has been claimed, he manages to obtain the illusion that the retinal image does change in size merely because an object is moved away from him. Some doubts are cast on this theory by Bower's research claiming to show that young infants (aged 2 to 20 weeks) when taught to respond to a large square shape and not to a small square shape, shown at the same distance, responded to the large square as though it were large even when it was moved to a distance such that the size of the retinal image was the same as that of the small square held at the original distance. The study suggests that size constancy may depend upon a mechanism built into the human nervous system rather than on learning. However, caution must be exercised in interpreting the results of this study because the technique used was a little crude. Also, the infants had had some experience in seeing their mothers move away from them and approach them, with corresponding changes in the size of the image.

In connection with the discussion of analyzers in the brain, the point has already been made that specific kinds of information analyzers have been identified in lower animals, and that in the frog a series of analyzers has been demonstrated to exist. Muntz (1964), reviewing some of the other work in this area, points out that similar analyzers have been identified in fish, rabbits, and pigeons. In these animals the analyzers studied have been located in the retina and optic nerve. He also notes that in many animals the specific analyzers respond only to very specific pieces of information. The male stickleback has a perceptual mechanism that prompts a response to the red spot of the female. Very distorted facsimiles of the female will be responded to, so long as the facsimiles carry the red spot. A realistic model of the female that does not have the red spot will be ignored by the male. Another classic example is the duckling which shows a panic reaction when a model of a short-necked hawk is moved overhead along a string, but shows no panic response when the direction of flight is reversed. These kinds of evidence are mentioned here to indicate that the nervous systems of lower organisms recognize form through the operation of analyzers of specific features of the visual input. That such analyzers do exist suggests that they may represent the general type of mechanism through which visual information at all evolutionary levels is analyzed. This hypothesis fits very well with knowledge of perception derived from psychological experiments with humans.

A final point to note is that in much of the British literature, the information analyzers are referred to as *filters*. The idea is that the analyzers allow a particular class of information to be filtered through to higher levels of the nervous system. Whether they are called filters or analyzers, the essential idea is the same.

Implications for the Design of Educational Materials

This chapter has been concerned with the processes involved in recognition. Although recognition is not a sufficient condition for learning, it would appear to be a desirable condition. The main implication of the knowledge presented for the design of audiovisual materials is one of providing cautions. The knowledge makes clear that many of the assumptions made in the design of materials need to be more carefully scrutinized than they have been in the past.

One important fact which has been stressed is that the person inspecting his environment would appear to have a choice between a broad inspection with little attention to detail or an inspection of a much more limited aspect of the environment examined at a much greater level of detail. Perhaps there are intermediate stages between these extremes. Most audiovisual materials do not reflect a design which has taken into account the possibility that the student has this kind of choice. But unless the attention of the student is properly directed, he is likely to function ineffectively in the learning situation. If the student concentrates on some minor detail when he is supposed to be scanning the entire screen and deriving some general impression, he may end up learning trivia. The same is true if he surveys the entire visual presentation when he should be examining carefully some central feature. To some extent the auditory channel can be used to provide information to control the student's attention, but little is known about how effective this channel is. One can reasonably assume that very complex visual displays, such as are provided by most films, encourage the viewer to scan a large amount of the information presented, but at a very crude level of analysis.

When an attempt is made to restrict the attention of the viewer to a particular aspect of a display, the problem is that of ensuring that he will structure his perception into figure and ground in the way required. Since there are not only differences between individuals in the way they structure the same display, but also differences in the way the same individual structures it on different occasions, the problem is not a simple one. The easiest way of ensuring that a particular object will become the figure and that the rest will merge into the background is to eliminate features of the background and present the part to be designated as figure on a uniform gray field. This is not often done by film producers, who like to provide an appropriate natural setting for the object that is the focus of interest. The effect of such a complex background on the understanding of the object that is the center of interest needs to be investigated.

Finally, the point needs to be made that man, like all complex organisms, is well designed for the purpose of monitoring what is going on in his environment without retaining much of what he observes. He likes to watch a changing scene as an end in itself, and only under exceptional circumstances is he likely to retain much of what happens in that scene. Indeed, he will not analyze the information in any great detail unless it fails in some way to meet his expectancies, either through a common event occurring in an unusual context or through the occurrence of some novel event. Man engages in watching and monitoring his environment or, as we say, he engages in experiencing, because he comes from a long line of living creatures that survived because they were watchful of the happenings in their environment. Man is designed to engage continuously in this game of watching what is going on, and so it is hardly surprising that children will remain in their seats, even hours at a time, watching the moving picture on a screen. This kind of *watching,* or *experiencing,* highly enjoyable though it is, should not be confused with *learning.* Man is much too efficiently designed to retain information about everything he sees and hears, but he will retain information only under quite exceptional circumstances.

Chapter 4

The Capacity of the Human Information System

In order to discuss many of the problems raised in this chapter, some additional concepts from information theory must be introduced. These concepts will provide a language permitting the discussion of the problems with more precision than is possible with common language, though perhaps still not with the precision to which one should aspire.

The Transmission of a Message

The term *information* as it is used in the context of information theory is only indirectly related to the layman's usage of the same term. For the laymen *information* generally signifies "knowledge," and knowledge is communicated through "meaningful statements," but information theory does not necessarily have anything to do with the communication of either meaning or knowledge as these are commonly conceptualized.

Information theory has a background in communication engineering and mathematical statistics. Engineers have long been faced with the problem of how much information can be transmitted over a particular channel such as a telephone line, and statisticians have had a parallel problem of how much information can be contained in a statistic such as a mean or standard deviation, and both have had to devise ways of determining the amount of information involved. One cannot help being surprised that these two very different problems happen to have very closely related solutions, but it was not until Shannon's "A Mathematical Theory of Communication" (1949) that the common nature of these problems began to be apparent. The Shannon paper was to have tremendous impact not only in the area of communication engineering, which was its context, but also on the behavioral sciences, where it began to provide a language for discussing problems which could not have been readily discussed before. However, the essential model on which information theory is based is the engineering model represented in Figure 4.

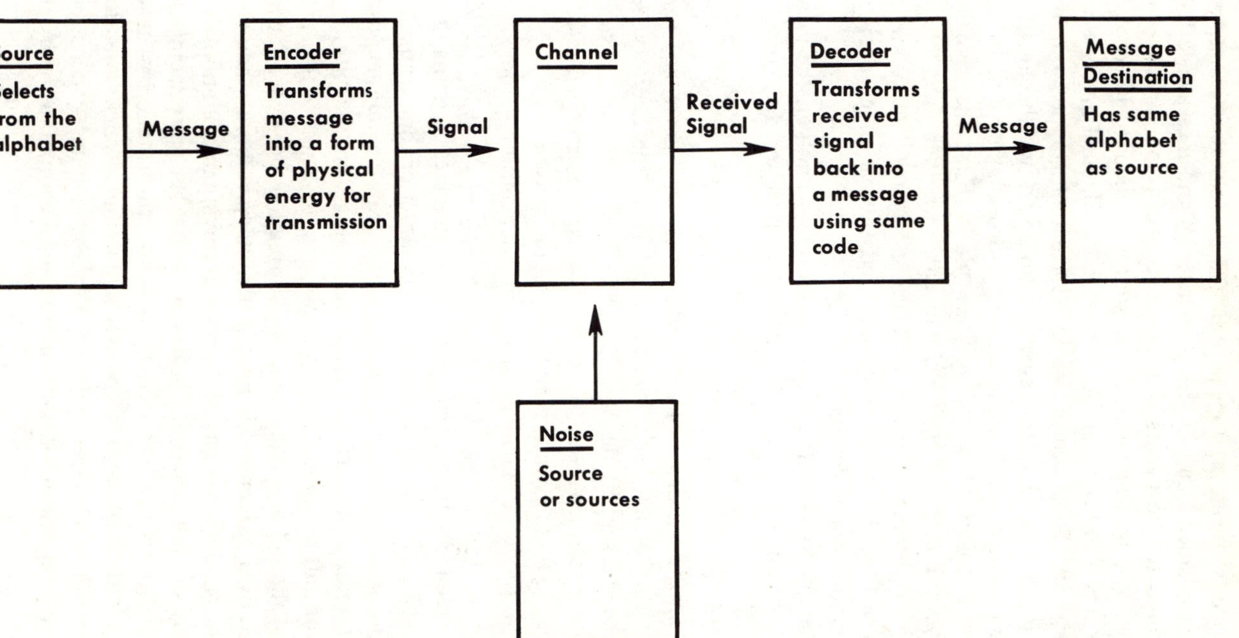

Figure 4. An information-transmission system.

The model shows a message source and a message destination, but before we consider some of the properties of the message, attention must be paid to the events that occur between the source and the destination. The message leaving the source is encoded in some form which permits it to be transmitted through the channel involved in the communication. Thus a message in Morse code tapped out by an operator is first encoded into electrical impulses which can then be transmitted along a line. In the case of Morse signals sent by radio, two different forms of encoding take place. First the signals are encoded into bursts of electrical current, and then later they are encoded into modulated radio waves. Some systems of communication require that the message be encoded several times during the entire communication sequence.

When one person communicates by speech to another, the message leaving the brain is first encoded into nerve impulses that control the mechanisms involved in the emission of speech. The message is then re-encoded into vibrations of the atmosphere which, in turn, produce vibrations in the ear drum of a potential recipient. Then the message is changed into a new code for transmission up the auditory nerve. Finally, the message is decoded at some high level in the nervous system by the recipient, and the original message is reconstructed in a form similar to that in which it appeared in the source.

Figure 4 shows a single channel for transmitting a message. A channel may have a large or a small capacity. A single telephone line has a much smaller capacity for transmitting messages than does a television channel. A laser beam has a still larger channel capacity for transmitting information and could, indeed, carry simultaneously as much information as can all the radio stations in the world. The concepts of information theory permit one to make quite precise statements about how many bits of information per second can be transmitted by a particular channel. Attempts have been made also to estimate the channel capacity of a person receiving information.

Channels do not transmit information without introducing some extraneous disturbance, referred to as *noise*. Information is orderly, in contrast with noise, which consists of random events. This definition of noise is not to be confused with the popular conception of noise as some unpleasant sound. In terms of information theory noise is not necessarily unpleasant and, indeed, whether it is unpleasant or pleasant is an irrelevant issue. When one is attempting to follow the words of one person against a background buzz of hundreds of persons talking simultaneously, the background buzz corresponds closely to this definition of noise. For the purposes of experimentation, devices have been built which will produce auditory noise at any level of intensity desired. Sometimes noise is used to *mask* messages, as in the device which produces a noise so that a person attempting to sleep will not be distracted by such message material as the radio next door, the conversation in the hall, and so forth. If noise is sufficiently loud, it may mask messages completely.

Although common language speaks of noise as being an auditory phenomenon, any sensory input can be accompanied by noise. One can as readily talk of visual noise as of auditory noise. An example of a visual input with a great amount of noise is that of a television screen in which the picture is partly masked by random flecks of light, known as snow. Such a picture is a "noisy" picture, just as a conversation held against a background of din is a noisy auditory communication.

Humans do not like to receive messages against a background of noise. A person may be able to follow extremely well a football game he is viewing on television despite the fact that the picture is quite noisy. Even though the information about the game is being well received by him, in the sense that he knows exactly what is going on, he may turn off the set because the noise bothers him. Noise in a human system does far more than simply make it difficult to receive the message.

The source transmits a message in terms of what is called an *alphabet*. This is not an alphabet in the ordinary sense of the term, but a set of alternatives in terms of which the message may be constructed. Any set of signs may be used for this purpose—letters, dots and dashes, dots alone, numbers—but the source and the receiver must use the same alphabet. A chain of selected items from the alphabet constitutes a message. Thus, within the framework of the theory, a source may transmit a series of signs selected from an alphabet, and at the message destination the same set of signs may be successfully reconstructed; but the question of whether or not the signs are meaningful is not a pertinent one as far as information theory is concerned.

An earlier chapter pointed out that information reduces uncertainty in the receiver and that the unit of information, the bit, is the amount of information which will reduce uncertainty by a particular amount. In a two-choice situation, the reception of one bit of information will resolve the uncertainty.

One additional point has to be understood concerning the relationship between the amount of information required to make a choice and the number of choices. Although one bit of information is needed to make a choice (and remove uncertainty) in a two-choice situation, only three bits of information are needed to resolve uncertainty in an eight-choice situation. This is readily understood by considering a game in which one person thinks of one of the first eight letters in the alphabet and the other person has to find out which letter it is by asking questions to which he receives an answer of "Yes" or "No." If the guesser goes about this task efficiently, he will have to ask only three questions. First, he will ask whether the letter in mind is among the first four or the second four letters. Then he will ask whether it is among the first two letters or the second two letters of the four-letter group. Once he has narrowed down the choice to two letters, his next question will permit him to determine which of the two letters it is. Thus three questions with Yes-No answers, each carrying one bit of information, will determine which one of the eight letters is the correct one. In other words, the solution to an eight-choice problem requires three bits of information. By extending the same argument one can show that a sixteen-choice problem requires four bits of information. One can generalize and say that an N-choice problem requires $\log_2 N$ bits of information in order to solve it.

Most messages delivered in words are quite repetitive. Consider the statement, "He was a fine man before he died." In a subtle way this statement makes several assertions twice. The words "he" and "man" both tell the listener that a male is involved. The words "was" and "died" both imply that the events referred to happened in the past. The words in the sentence are quite repetitive in the meaning they convey, and some can be crossed out without obscuring the meaning. The three words "fine man died," convey almost as much meaning as did the original eight words. In composing a telegram, one usually cuts out all the words that have repetitive meaning to leave the message short and concise. In technical terms, one does not speak of a message as "being repetitive," but as *containing redundancy*.

With the aid of information-theory measures, it is now possible to measure the amount of redundancy in a stimulus sequence, in some cases. Shannon (1949) has suggested a method by which we can measure the redundancy of letter sequences. His method was to present a series of letters and spaces, and then ask the subjects to guess which letter went in each space in sequence. As the subject guesses correctly, the letters are entered in the spaces. When he guesses incorrectly, one of two different techniques is used: (1) The experimenter may tell the subject what the right response should be, or (2) the experimenter may ask the subject to keep on guessing until the correct response is made and the number of errors are recorded. An example of this kind of task would be a set of 16 spaces. If the subject tediously guessed that the first letters or blank spaces to be inserted were ONCE UPO   , it would be very easy for him to insert the remainder of the letters correctly and to come up with the phrase ONCE UPON A TIME. Thus, if he were able to arrive at the first eight letters and spaces by pure guesswork, he could then enter the remaining entries correctly without any prompting. This would mean that the message had a 50 per cent redundancy; that is to say, one has to know only 50 per cent of the message in order to know the complete message.

Ordinary English has a high degree of redundancy. In most prose one can cut out half the message without any loss for comprehension, for the reader can fill in the missing parts correctly. What the writer of a telegram does is to cut out all the redundant words which would ordinarily be there but which are unnecessary for the understanding of the message. Telegram writing is possible in its typical clipped form because English is so redundant. This raises the interesting question of why English, or any other language, evolved in such an inefficient form. One suggested reason is that most speech is sloppy in enunciation and that redundancy is necessary to make it intelligible.

The redundancy of speech is a matter of considerable practical interest in view of the evidence to be discussed later that the elimination of some redundancy in instructional materials may increase the effectiveness with which the student utilizes his time.

The application of information theory to the study of language as a communication system has led to important developments, such as ways of increasing the amount of verbal communication that can be undertaken in a given interval of time. One can, for example, omit numerous small sections (3/100 second or less) from speech recorded on tape and end up with less recorded material than one had in the first place. The speech can then be played in less time than was needed to play the original. Such compressed versions of speech communicate more information in less time than the original versions and also produce more effective learning for each minute spent on them. Speeded speech of this kind, known as *compressed speech,* is produced by reducing the amount of redundancy.

Less developed are applications to the analysis of visual materials, although a beginning has been made in studies of what makes shapes appear to be complex rather than simple. Rappaport (1957) explored a similar problem in a series of four studies of the effect of redundancy on the ability to discriminate visual forms. Adding redundancy to a form did not improve its recognizability. However, Rappaport also introduced visual noise into the presentations of the patterns, which had the effect of making their outlines less clear-cut. When he did this, he found that redundancy improved recognizability. This is very similar to what occurs in the case of auditory communications. When we are speaking over a "good" telephone line, we can mumble our words, as we usually do, and the message is still understood at the other end. But when the telephone line is noisy, we increase the redundancy by carefully enunciating each component of each word. Redundancy becomes important when the channel becomes noisy. Rappaport also points out that excessive redundancy may be harmful to the recognition of visual form. The latter is very much like enunciating each sound fully and slowly over a telephone line. If this is done to extremes, then the message becomes difficult to interpret.

A point brought out by the Rappaport study is that the *amount* of information in a display is not the only factor that makes for ease of information reception. The manner of *organization* of the information is of critical importance. Also, redundancy, and particularly redundancy in the form of symmetry, does not help the receiver as much as one might perhaps have anticipated.

The Capacity of the Perceptual System

The concept of channel capacity derived from the description of physical systems can also be applied to human beings. In humans, *channel capacity* generally refers to the amount of information that the human can process as determined by the physiological and psychological limits inherent in him or the situation. The concept of channel capacity, in relation to the human information system, has been used with a number of quite distinct meanings. Sometimes it has been used to refer to the capacity of the sense organs. Sometimes it has been used to refer to the capacity of the sensory nerves carrying information to the brain—a capacity that may vary at different levels of the nervous system. In other studies, channel capacity refers to the capacity of the higher centers to utilize information. A variety of meanings is probably necessary since the information channel within the human subject is certainly not a system of uniform capacity. An additional source of confusion in this entire area is caused by the fact that the term channel capacity sometimes refers to the amount of information that can be taken in from an instantaneous presentation and sometimes to the rate at which information can be transmitted and utilized. The former is measured in bits, and the latter in terms of bits per second.

Let us begin by considering the information capacity at the level of the receptors, keeping in mind that this may not be a good indicator of the capacity of the system at higher levels. It is important at this point to make a distinction familiar to engineers between the information capacity of the sense channel, which is usually measured in bits per second, and the information content of the signals transmitted. Consider, for example, a parallel problem in the transmission of television signals. A television channel has a capacity for transmitting information at about 5.7×10^6 bits per second, but the signal it transmits may carry only a very small amount of information, as when the station identification is broadcast at times that the station is not operating. The mere fact that a sensory channel has a large capacity for handling information does not mean that it transmits large amounts of information.

Most of the knowledge available concerning the information-handling capacity of the sense organs is derived from the study of the eye and the ear. Since these organs are of primary importance for information transmission in schools, a brief review of their capacities and the immediate afferent nerves which lead from them is appropriate.

Information capacity of the retina and optic nerve. The information-handling capacity of the eye is directly related to the problem of visual acuity, which is normally measured by determining the number of discriminations which the eye can make. Jacobson (1951a), utilizing data from a number of sources, concludes that the retina functions as an information-transmitting device as though it consisted of a grid of 240,000 squares. He infers further that the number of stimuli within each square of the grid which can be discriminated per second is 18. From this, he concludes that the information capacity of the eye is $18 \times 240,000$ bits per second which amounts to 4.32×10^6

bits per second. The argument involves many assumptions which cannot be explored or even stated here, but it may be said that the estimate is probably on the conservative side. An example of a simplifying assumption used by Jacobson is that the transmission is achromatic. Color adds a coding dimension which, in turn, contributes to the information capacity of the visual channel as he has estimated it.

Information capacity of the ear. Jacobson (1951b) has also attempted to provide data which compares the information capacity of the eye and ear. The possible combinations of frequency and intensity of tones which lie within the range that the ear can perceive indicate that the ear could transmit up to 10,000 bits per second. The latter figure is a rough estimate and, as in the case of estimating the information-transmitting capacity of the retina and optic nerve, involves a number of assumptions which cannot be fully justified.

If the estimates of Jacobson can be considered to represent the general order of the information-carrying capacity of the two perceptual systems, then, in theory, the eye may carry 430 times as much information per unit of time as can the ear. A part of this difference is to be accounted for by the fact that the optic nerve has about 900,000 fibers, while the auditory nerve as it leaves the cochlea has only about 30,000. In addition, Jacobson suggests that each optic fiber may carry about 5 bits of information per second, while the auditory nerve fibers are limited to about 0.3 bits per second. This comparison of the two sets of fibers may appear on the surface to account for differences in the information capacity of the two modalities, but the comparison is based on the assumption that both nerve tracts use a binary coding system whereas the auditory tract does not. The two tracts differ in the extent to which fibers function independently from one another; the optic nerve fibers show the greater independence.

The data discussed here do *not* lead to the conclusion that a greater quantity of *useful* information can be supplied through the human eye than through the human ear. It is quite conceivable that the same verbal communication by written and spoken words may involve a much larger information capacity when it is transmitted by the eye than by the ear. Also, one can easily understand how the image of a table requires a greater channel capacity than does the word "table" for effective transmission. What is much more important is the fact that the brain is capable of utilizing at the highest levels less than 1 per cent of the information provided by the ear and perhaps only 1 part in 250,000 for the eye. An understanding of what aspects of the information are utilized and of how the messages communicated become compressed is important for the problem of designing messages in such a way that the nervous system will retain the essential information and discard the irrelevant.

Another problem is that of determining the information capacity of what we have called the perceptual field (distinguishing it from the preperceptual field). The studies considered in this category have generally attempted to determine the amount of information that can be instantaneously grasped from the trace system, and *not* the rate at which information can continuously flow into the system. The studies considered here are very similar to those that in former eras were referred to as studies of the *span of attention.* In the latter kind of investigation, a number of letters or digits were briefly displayed to the subject, who then had to recall what had appeared. The subject was thus required to read off as much of the information as he could from the stimulus trace before it faded.

In a classic paper by Miller (1956) entitled "The Magical Number 7, Plus or Minus Two: Some Limits on Our Capacity for Processing Information," the theme was developed that the perceptual system has a limited capacity for processing information. The basic studies cited by Miller involved the categorization of information along a single dimension. Miller's essential argument was that when a person has to make some absolute judgment about a stimulus, he is able to judge it in terms of a scale involving about seven categories. Miller introduces this concept by referring to an experiment in which subjects were asked to classify tones which ranged from about two octaves below middle C to about four octaves above. Subjects were first taught to assign numbers to tones. For example, the highest tone might be called "1," a tone in the middle of the scale "2," and the lowest tone "3." Then, when further tones were sounded, subjects would have to identify each as a "1" tone, a "2" tone, or a "3" tone. With only three categories, this was a very simple task for the subjects to do. So long as subjects were asked to classify only four or five tones spread over the six octaves, there was no difficulty in assigning the tones to the right categories. When five categories were used, subjects began to make mistakes. From then on, performance began to trail off, with most subjects able to use about six categories and no more. When a greater number of categories was used, this merely resulted in a greater number of errors, for subjects continued to behave as though they could use only about six categories. The input permits the receiver to make a six-alternative choice. Information permitting a six-alternative choice provides 2.5 bits of information. This number represents the capacity to draw information from an immediate presentation, which is what Miller referred to as channel capacity. Miller cited a number of studies showing that channel capacity, as he defined it, varied around the figure 2.6 bits, with some variation up and down. For example, he cited studies in which channel capacity for absolute judgments of pitch was estimated at 2.5; for absolute judgments of loudness, 2.3 bits; for taste intensities, 1.9 bits; and for judgments of visual position, 3.25 bits.

There is a surprising amount of agreement between the channel capacities of the different dimensions as measured in this way. One should keep in mind, however, that the differences in the channel capacities of the different dimensions are probably not of real significance. Also, there is considerable variation from one dimension to another, although not as much as one might at first suspect.

Other experiments have used two dimensions at the same time. In examining everyday experiences with communication, we see that one is able to make absolute judgments about more than just seven different categories of objects, discriminating between them with confidence. One reason for this ability, that might seem to be at odds with the channel capacities derived by the method described above, is that one may be reacting to more than just one dimension of the object. There are many different dimensions along which an object (stimulus) could vary. One may obtain an additive effect when two or more dimensions are varied simultaneously in the same class of objects. Thus, one may think of colors as falling into about seven broad categories (red, green, blue, and so on), and one may think of fabrics as falling into seven categories on a roughness-fineness dimension, but a combination of roughness and color gives 7×7 categories.

Research has shown that the adding of dimensions does indeed increase channel capacity, but not as much as might be expected from the channel capacities of the different dimensions considered separately and as measured by the method previously outlined. For example, when Pollack (1953) asked listeners to judge both the loudness and the pitch of pure tones (loudness has a channel capacity of 2.3 bits; pitch, 2.5 bits), one could expect a channel capacity for the combined effects of these two dimensions to be 4.8 bits, namely, the sum of the two separate channel capacities. The experimental results show a channel capacity of 3.1 bits, instead. The addition of dimensions augments the channel capacity for making absolute judgments, but not as much as one might expect from the capacities of the individual channels alone. Studies of a two-dimensional array of stimuli are a far cry from the complex stimuli of the real world faced every day. A study by Pollack and Ficks (1954) attempted to deal with very complex variables. They used six different acoustic variables that they could change: frequency, intensity, rate of interruption, on-time fraction, total duration, and spatial location. Each one of these six variables could assume any one of five different values; so altogether there were 5^6 (15,625) different tones that they could present. Under these conditions, the transmitted information was 7.2 bits, which means that there were 150 different categories that could be identified with minimal error.

The studies briefly reported here may be summarized by saying that the addition of stimulus dimensions results in an increase in the channel capacity, but that the capacities for the separate dimensions do not summate. As more dimensions are added, there is a decreasing increment in the channel capacity for each new dimension added. People are less accurate in any one dimension if they must judge more than one attribute at the same time.

The data suggest that the amount of information which can be utilized from a single presentation of a display is probably quite limited—perhaps of the order of 10 bits. However, since most displays that are introduced in educational settings are shown to the learner for extended periods involving many minutes, the limitation is not as great as it may seem. Furthermore, the kinds of studies cited by Miller involve information that is perceptually analyzed at a high level of detail. In many learning tasks involving audiovisual materials, only a very crude level of analysis is expected. In a film of folk dancers in Switzerland, the learner may be expected to gain little more than a general impression, perhaps also noting certain specific features pointed out to him before the film showing.

Finally, it is of interest that the data summarized by Miller and briefly cited here, derived from absolute-judgment experiments, fit very closely with data derived from two other, very different sources. First, there is the kind of data that psychologists have derived from using rating scales. From such data they have learned that most raters can use a rating scale involving about seven categories. If the rating scale involves more than seven categories, the rater does not provide more information. Thus the use of a single rating scale can provide somewhere between 2.5 and 3.0 bits of information per rating but not any more. The channel of the rater appears to be able to handle this amount of information, but that is all. A second source of data comes from what have been termed span-of-attention experiments. A typical form of this type of experiment is that in which a number of digits are flashed on a screen. In the case of adults, approximately seven digits can be recalled from such a momentary presentation, and much the same is found when the digits are spoken at about two or three a second. As Miller points out, the magic number 7 also turns up here, suggesting once more but in a different context that the human adult can use about seven categories of things at one time. Neisser (1967) points out that many psychologists derive from these data the idea that what we have called the perceptual system is very much like a system having a limited number of pigeonholes into each of which a single chunk of information can be placed. These pigeonholes are called *slots*. After a person attempting to perceive digits from a momentary presentation has filled his seven slots, he has no place left in which to temporarily store more digits, and hence he cannot recognize any more for he has no place in which to store them temporarily. The slot theory is attractive, but it is not widely accepted partly because there are data which do not fit it and partly because it is a very crude theory.

The problem we have just considered is the amount of information that the human perceptual system can use from a single and static presentation of information. Another and related problem is the capacity of the system to process information continuously. From the single-presentation studies, one derives an answer that the human perceptual system can utilize about 2.5 bits at a time. The answer is in *bits,* but if we wanted to know the capacity of the system to process information on a continuous basis, then the answer would have to be given in *bits per second,* that is, the amount of information per unit of time that the system can handle. In deriving an estimate for information processing at the higher levels of the nervous system, it is important to keep in mind that the search should not be for a unique solution. It seems quite clear that one can receive far more information on a receive-and-forget basis than one can on a receive-and-store basis. The estimates available to date are of the former rather than the latter type.

In considering this problem, Jacobson (1951b) suggests that if a person were to receive speech at the rate of 300 words per minute, and if both the speaker and the receiver were equipped with a vocabulary of 150,000 words, then the transmission rate would be estimated to be about 90 bits of information per second. Since the latter rate does not take into account the redundancy feature of spoken English, which is fairly high, the true transmission rate of information might be estimated at around 50 bits per second. This would require only one-half of 1 per cent of the channel capacity of the sensory system at the level of the auditory nerve. If the entire redundant message were transmitted, then it would utilize only about 1 per cent of the capacity of the system. Jacobson makes another computation which suggests that the information transmitted by a piece of music is at the rate of about 78 bits per second. If such speech and musical transmissions represent messages of the maximum amount of information which the brain can utilize, then one must conclude that the brain is capable of using somewhat less than 1 per cent of the information that the auditory mechanism is capable of transmitting.

An analysis similar to that of Jacobson was made by Quastler and Wulff (1955), who came up with the figure of 25 bits per second for continuous reception of speech. These researchers also had to make assumptions about the redundancy of speech, the time necessary to receive a component of speech, and the limitations of the alphabet of the receiver and the sender.

Pierce and Karlin (1957) estimated the "information rate of the human channel" by asking subjects to read aloud words as rapidly as possible. What they really did was to measure the information output of the system, and this they concluded to be about 43 bits per second —a figure that is in line with the other estimates made by other means. However, the information capacity of the human perceptual system is probably larger than that derived from an estimate based on the output of the system, for the fact is well established that one can read far more rapidly than one can speak. Reading of straightforward material is generally at least 50 per cent faster than speech.

Fogel (1967) cites a study in which the input of information was slowly increased in a series of tasks, such as playing sequences of notes, striking keys on the typewriter, and doing simple arithmetical problems. On such tasks, when the rate of presenting notes, or letters, or arithmetic problems increased, the rate of making the responses tended to increase. This means that as the amount of information concerning which keys to strike increased, the subject showed a corresponding increase in his ability to receive and use information. However, when the rate at which the subject was provided with information increased beyond a certain point, performance tended to fall off and the individual's ability to process information also declined. The peak of performance was at about 25 bits per second; but when information was supplied at a faster rate, the amount of information processed by the individual declined. If a person is flooded with more information than he can handle, his performance becomes quite ineffective. In a number of studies of learning nonsense syllables that some of my students and I conducted some years ago, it was found that when the syllables were flashed on a screen at an excessively fast rate, the subjects did not make a reasonable adjustment and begin by learning, say, the first and last syllables. They failed to learn a single syllable. Snow the learner with information, and he does not separate out a little piece of the task for learning. He may learn nothing.

The studies cited give no direct indication of what might be the rate at which a person is able to place material in permanent memory. If one assumes that a person can perceive, hold in temporary storage, and then discard information at a maximum rate of about 50 bits per second, it is clear that the amount that can be placed in permanent memory is much less. A first-grade child building a reading-recognition vocabulary generally has to be exposed to a word at least 25 times before he can be expected to recognize the word readily. This finding would lead us to the position that permanent storage is 25 times as slow as short-term storage and would point to the conclusion that the rate at which information can be placed in permanent memory is perhaps no higher than 2 bits per second. Perhaps an adult can place information in permanent storage at three or four times this rate, though some of the increasing rate from childhood to adult life must be a result of the fact that the adult is generally confronted with the task of storing information that is redundant with information already stored. For example, a friend says that his address is on Surrey Street. Since one is already familiar with the name "Surrey," one only has to hook up this information already stored with the name of one's friend, which is also stored. Most of the task of the adult in storing what he believes to be new information is actually the linking together of information already stored.

The general picture of the information capacity of the perceptual systems can be represented by a funnel, with a very large capacity for receiving information at the receiving end and a narrow neck at the other which greatly restricts the flow. This is why we see and hear much, but are unable to use more than a small amount of what we see and hear. This characteristic of the information system has important implications for the design of instructional materials, which may easily flood the perceptual systems with information but provide no assurance that the small fraction of crucially important information is ever processed to the point where it becomes stored in permanent memory. Indeed, one may be exposed to an instructional motion picture and come away only with the knowledge that one's visual system has been exposed to an overwhelming experience, but that is all. A major part of the function of the designer of such motion pictures is to attempt to arrange the presentation so that the important features are noted and retained. This can be done in a number of ways. One way is to design the movie so that only the important features of whatever it presents are visible. Another is to use the sound track to provide cues to the learner concerning what he is to perceive and what he is to ignore. A third approach is to provide such cues before the picture is shown. Nothing is known about the virtues of each of these ways of helping the perceiver to utilize his limited-capacity perceptual system to maximum advantage.

Development of Perceptual-System Capacity

Very little information is available in the literature on the capacity of the perceptual systems at different ages. In the past few years, the author together with a number of other research workers has been conducting some studies of this problem. The general trend of the evidence is that the capacity of the perceptual systems of children in the lower elementary grades is substantially less than that of the adult and that it shows a steady increment with age. The child is also much less capable of identifying the relevant information in a complex display. A child first shown a picture for a very short flash on repeated occasions is very likely to latch his attention on some minor feature of the picture and to recognize nothing else, even though the picture is shown ten or more times. In contrast, the older child in a similar situation slowly changes his report of what he sees on repeated exposures to the picture, as he slowly sifts out the significant from the insignificant features.

The Relative Efficiency of Vision and Hearing

The large channel capacity of the eye and optic-nerve system permits the inclusion of dimensions, such as space dimensions, about which the auditory system can provide little information. A large channel capacity of a sensory system does not, in itself, provide an advantage over a sensory system with a smaller channel capacity, for the higher centers of the brain are limited in the amount of information they can use at any one time. The advantage lies in the dimensions that are opened up through a large capacity. This becomes clear when we leave the field of physiology and consider the relative effectiveness of the eye and the ear for handling communications.

Studies of the relative efficiency of the visual and auditory modes for the transmission of information have been typically undertaken in research, not in educational settings, but in settings where the problem has been to find ways of communicating efficiently with the operator of a piece of equipment. In such studies the operator most commonly mentioned is the aircraft pilot or the equipment operator. A point stressed in many studies is that the efficiency of a particular perceptual system for transmitting information depends upon the immediate task faced by the operator. For example, there are times when the pilot of an aircraft is fully occupied with visually watching the radio compass and panel instruments, as well as locating other flying aircraft. At such times, additional information must be transmitted through the ear. When two-way communication is needed, this has to be accomplished by auditory means since two-way visual communication is a much less well developed art.

In addition, one cannot reasonably ask the general question whether the eye or the ear is more efficient for the transmission of information, since clearly some information is better transmitted by one sensory channel than by another. If a person needed to know about the appearance or physical characteristics of an unfamiliar animal, he would do much better to examine the animal visually than to hear a description related by another observer. Such visual observation would be best until he wanted to know about the vocal noises emitted by the animal, in which case he would do better to hear the actual sound of the animal than to obtain visual information about the vocal mechanism. Where direct information is needed about the world, the sensory modality should be used which can best transmit directly the particular physical information involved.

The problem of the relative efficiency of the auditory and visual systems becomes meaningful when the same information can be coded in two different ways—one appropriate for transmission through the ear, and the other through the eye. This problem has been more often recognized as an important one in the design of aircraft cockpits than in the design of audiovisual devices. For example, a warning signal for a pilot may be provided either by the flashing of a light or by the sounding of an alarm. The problem in such a case is to determine which one of the two warning signals is the more efficient. A special case of this class of problem is found in the use of language which can be transmitted through both the eye and the ear in the form of spoken or written material, and this special case has important implications for education.

A summary has been made by Chapanis (1965) of the information available concerning the relative efficiency of the visual and the auditory channels for data presentation. A good place to begin this discussion is to point out that when coded information is used, there are difficulties in making a comparison of visual and auditory presentations. For example, the same information may be coded so that it involves a color discrimination in the visual modality and a pitch discrimination in the auditory modality. This coding raises the question of whether pitch and color discriminations are comparable. Perhaps the visual system would be more effective if the same information were coded so that it involved a brightness discrimination, in which case a brightness discrimination would be compared with a pitch discrimination. Again, when verbal material is transmitted through either the eye or the ear, the auditory system involves the perception of a modulated sound wave while the visual channel involves form perception and the stimulus has primarily spatial characteristics. Here again, one does not know whether this comparison is an optimum one. There is the possibility that if printing involved the use of differences in shading and hue in addition to the spatial qualities of ordinary type, then the transmission of information would be much better than it is at present.

The relative efficiency of inputs through different perceptual systems depends upon other conditions, such as the character of the other activities in which the receiver is engaged at the particular time. For example, if the task of a pilot required him at a particular time to be scanning the space in front of him, looking for the lights at the approach to the runway, inputs of information from the control tower should not provide visual displays which he can only observe by redirecting this vision from the direction of the windshield to the direction of the instrument panel.

Chapanis points out that there is advantage in using a visual presentation when the message is involved and complex, and has to be referred to several times. The term *referability* is used in this connection to indicate the extent to which a display of information presents data for a relatively long duration so that the receiver can refer to it repeatedly to guide his external or internal behavior. Very few auditory messages are referable in this sense, though apparatus can be rigged so that a receiver can obtain repetition of any particular communication. Many kinds of visual transmissions have the characteristics of referability, though under most circumstances motion-picture and television transmissions do not. Such lack of referability is a serious weakness in the value of these media as educational devices. In contrast, in the classroom, repetitions of auditory information as well as of visual displays are easily arranged. The visual system is also of advantage when the message is long, when it involves spatial orientation (as in giving directions for getting somewhere), or when the environment is noisy and an auditory message might be lost (as in some classrooms). Visual communications may also be advantageously used when the receiver's auditory channel is overloaded, as when he is listening to music and one wants him to attend to particular features of the music by pointing to the score. Auditory messages, on the other hand, are particularly useful when the immediate attention of the learner must be obtained. These are all good points to note, but some additional guidance in the choice between the auditory and the visual channels for communicating information are provided in Henneman and Long (1954), which also has some relevance for the design of audiovisual materials.

The literature searched by Henneman and Long consists of studies which have made comparisons with respect to specific aspects of the visual and the auditory systems, but not studies of the relative efficiency of the modalities when complex tasks are involved. The comparisons in these studies fall into the following categories.

The fact that only the eye and not the ear has any directional orientation in man has the important consequence that the eye can be moved to receive or not to receive stimuli while the ear cannot.

Certain auditory stimuli, such as high-pitched sounds, also have the capacity of forcing themselves on the perceptual system so that they cannot be ignored. Thus, in the design of a sound movie, a television program, or a television commercial, circumstances can be arranged so that the receiver can hardly escape from receiving the auditory message, but much less can be done to ensure that the video portion will be received. The receiver's gaze may simply be directed in the wrong direction. For this reason, transmissions of crucial information should be auditory rather than visual, except where there are very strong reasons for using the visual channel.

Dimensions for coding. Despite the fact that conditions for the transmission of information have to be much more carefully arranged to obtain the attention of viewers than to obtain the attention of hearers, much more has been done and probably can be done to devise ways of coding visual transmissions than of coding auditory transmissions. While auditory information is rarely coded in forms other than speech, Morse code, warning signals (such as automobile horns), and perhaps music, the coding of visual information includes a vast range of laboratory instruments as well as graphs, pictures, and other displays commonly found in books. Compare the sound on a tape with the visual material in a well-designed textbook to note the simplicity of the auditory presentation and the sophistication of the visual materials.

An important difference is also immediately apparent in the presentation of information through the two different systems. Visual information requires little more than paper and ink for storage and presentation, but the storage and subsequent presentation of auditory information requires rather complicated mechanical or electrical equipment.

The reason for the poverty of coding procedures in the auditory area as compared with the visual stems also from the fact that the latter provides a much greater number of dimensions than the former in terms of which information may be coded. Tradition may also play a part in the fact that the visual sense has been much better exploited than the auditory for the transmission of information, and this factor may be as important as the number of available dimensions in terms of which information may be coded.

The capacity of the eye to make use of spatial discriminations is far greater than that of the ear. Charts and diagrams as well as many common instruments, including the clock, take advantage of the capacity of the eye to make use of spatial characteristics. The capacity of the ear to make use of spatial relations is so limited that the properties of auditory space are rarely used for the transmission of information. The spatial quality of visual presentation makes it possible for a person to perform certain operations, such as the simultaneous comparison of two objects or sets of data or other displays. In the case of hearing, there is a tendency for one transmission to mask another, simultaneous transmission unless very special precautions are taken; but this confusion effect does not have to occur in the case of vision, for the displays can be spatially separated and still remain within the field of vision. There is even some possibility of superimposing visual messages without interference, as occurs with the color coding of different overlays or different parts of particular overlays.

While data can be presented to the eye either simultaneously or sequentially, data transmitted to the ear must generally be presented sequentially. While the ear does have some capacity for separating simultaneously presented messages, the difficulty of undertaking this task is such that the simultaneous presentation of two messages is rarely found except in the case of music. The issue of the relative efficiency of the two senses for the making of temporal discriminations has been studied, but the outcomes of the research are equivocal. Henneman and Long cite a study which shows that auditory Morse code can be received more rapidly than visual Morse code (but this may be a practice effect). However, other studies are also cited which point to the conclusion that vision and hearing are about equal for the detection of discrete stimuli.

The basic problem related to the use of the auditory and the visual channels is the relative efficiency of these channels for communicating material to be learned when identical information is transmitted by means of the two channels. The obvious material to use for such a study is in the verbal form. While other kinds of material, such as music, have comparable visual and auditory forms, there are relatively few persons who are practiced in the use of these other forms.

Many studies have been undertaken in which verbal material has been presented through the eye alone, the ear alone, and through both senses. The early studies, which generally involved simple materials presented at a single, specified rate, have been reviewed by Day and Beach (1950). The latter review covers research of questionable quality, and the fact is that most of the studies which have been undertaken appeared in the early part of the century with very few since 1940. The recent and related studies of Broadbent (1962, 1963), Triesman (1960), Cherry (1953), and others represent such a different technique and approach that they will be reviewed separately in a later chapter. In a sense, the latter studies have superseded those considered by Day and Beach.

In the studies which come within this review, the learning of four different kinds of materials are considered. These are nonsense syllables, digits, discrete words, and meaningful prose. The latter has sometimes been featured in studies of the effects of advertising, comparing auditory and visual methods of presenting the same material. Despite the fact that the studies cover a great diversity of materials, topics, and learning and retention conditions, Day and Beach consider that a number of generalizations emerge from them although many are based on very small samples and do not include tests of significance. These generalizations are summarized in the following paragraphs:

1. Meaningful, familiar material is presented more efficiently aurally, but relatively meaningless material is presented more efficiently visually. A number of different factors could be involved in this conclusion. When nonsense syllables are transmitted to a receiver, accurate transmission is more likely to occur with visual presentation since auditory presentations may involve some ambiguity. For example, the syllable BER is clear and unambiguous as written, but as spoken it could be mistaken for BUR or BIR. For this reason alone, meaningless material would be better transmitted by the visual channel. The results from which this generalization is derived are also contaminated by an age factor, and at lower age levels one might expect the difference to disappear.

2. The higher the ability level of the receiver, the greater is the advantage of a visual presentation. This effect may be due to the fact that those who obtain the highest scores on such receiving tasks tend to be the best readers.

3. The better the reading ability of the individual, the more effective becomes a visual presentation. This conclusion is inevitable since the visual presentations in the studies reviewed were all verbal.

4. The efficiency of a visual presentation increases with age. At the age of six, the visual presentation is inferior, but this inferiority vanishes by the age of sixteen. This effect may reflect the increase in

speed of reading which occurs with age. It suggests the importance of the learning factor in determining the relative efficiency of one channel over another in the transmission of information. A recent study by Cooper and Gaeth (1967) runs counter to this conclusion. These investigators found visual superiority for the presentation of nouns in Grades 4, 5, and 6, compared with Grades 10 and 12, and suggest that their findings reflect the habit systems of the individuals involved.

5. If the material is particularly difficult, it is more effectively received visually, whereas particularly easy material is better received auditorially. The relative effectiveness of the visual presentation increases as the material becomes more difficult. (This latter conclusion could be a result of the fact that visually presented material can be easily examined and reexamined, and much complex material may require more than a single presentation for comprehension.)

6. If comprehension is tested by immediate recall, a visual presentation provides the better recall; if the test of comprehension is made after a delay, an auditory presentation provides the more favorable condition for retention. (This conclusion lacks strength both in the amount of data cited in support and in the fact that it does not fit any particular set of expectations.)

7. The efficiency of a visual presentation, in contrast with an auditory presentation, diminishes as the delay recall is increased. (Here again, the relationship to delayed recall is a puzzling one, and most of the data which support this conclusion are the same as those which support the previous conclusion.)

8. One great advantage of the visual type of presentation system is the relatively greater referability, or opportunity for reviewing the material, that it affords; but the less the referability of the visual presentation, the less is its advantage over an auditory presentation. (This conclusion appears to provide an explanation of some of the preceding conclusions.)

9. Prose and meaningful information are better understood with an auditory presentation; material such as code that is comparatively discrete and nonredundant is more effectively received visually. The factor of referability may well be operating in this case also.

The type of research considered by Day and Beach has been a vanishing activity among psychologists, perhaps because of the attempt during the late 1950's to concentrate on research of complex materials such as sound motion pictures and educational television broadcasts. Such materials do not lend themselves well to the study of the relative efficiency of two perceptual systems for the transmission of information. Almost nothing could be found in more recent literature which followed up systematically the knowledge already gained from the studies reviewed by Day and Beach.

A second important factor which appears to come out of the review is that experience plays a very important role in determining the extent to which one perceptual system is superior to the other. While there appears to emerge from many of these studies the conclusion that with younger subjects the visual system is inferior to the auditory, this may be a product of the fact that the visual tasks involved in the studies have been typically verbal and required reading. Whether the same difference would occur with nonverbal and nonsymbolic visual representation is an open question.

Most of the studies in the Day and Beach review have utilized rather slow transmissions of both auditory and visual materials. In contrast, transmissions in daily life are typically quite fast. A reading speed of 300 words per minute is common, but one rarely hears a speaker who moves along at a rate much above 200 words per minute. Until recently there was no satisfactory way in which the words of speech could be presented at a rate comparable to that found in reading, in order to compare the efficiency of the two perceptual systems for communicating verbal information. One rather unsatisfactory way of providing auditory verbal material at rates comparable to visual, printed verbal materials is through making a record and speeding it up on playback. This method produces results that are considered disagreeable by most listeners, but it does increase the amount learned per unit of time of exposure. Another procedure is provided by a range of devices, known as speech compressors, that remove some of the redundancy of speech. What these most commonly do is to discard very small segments of the speech, but without leaving any gaps in the sound. This is done by running a taped recording through a device which simply skips over certain small segments of the tape. The omitted sections are generally of the order of a few hundredths of a second, and not sufficiently long to result in the omission of any single phoneme. What this does is to cut some of the redundancy in spoken speech, and tapes thus cut by as much as 50 per cent in total length provide speech that sounds rapid, but not otherwise distorted.

A review of studies of compressed speech by Jester and Travers (1966) indicates that the maximum learning per unit of time takes place for college sophomores when the material is run at an effective rate of about 300 words per minute. This is interesting in view of the fact that the same peak for reading efficiency occurs also at about 300 words per minute. The data thus suggest that with ordinary printed material and with corresponding spoken material the maximum information-processing rate is probably the same. This, in turn, suggests that the peak is set not by the sense organs, but by the higher centers, which analyze the information at a sophisticated level. The possibility exists that the visual, auditory, and haptic perceptual systems may all have approximately the same capacity for the analysis of information at the highest levels.

Redundancy can also be reduced in spoken and printed material by another means, the elimination of whole words. In most verbal communications there is substantial verbal redundancy. In a study by Allen and Travers (1967), the redundancy of spoken material was reduced by eliminating those words judged to contribute the least amount of independent information and then compressing the resulting cut text by the methods described above. The optimum combination was found when 20 per cent of the words were eliminated and the resulting spoken material was compressed to 40 per cent of the original time. The material thus spoken corresponded to a presentation rate of 400 words per minute, suggesting that eliminating unnecessary words may facilitate high-speed reception.

Work on compressed speech shows rather clearly that as much information can probably be communicated through the ear as through the eye in any given interval of time, despite the fact that the eye has a substantially larger channel capacity. The bottleneck in the information processing occurs "upstairs," in the brain, and both auditory and visual information seem to encounter either the same bottleneck or bottlenecks of equal size.

There is also some evidence that, when adults are presented with verbal material in both printed form and speech at the same time, and when the pace is that of rapid reading, these individuals choose between receiving the material visually or auditorially. They do not attempt to both read and listen. Under these conditions, typical behavior is to close the eyes and listen intently or to put the hands over the ears, blocking the sound, and to read the message. Some subjects show a preference for taking in the information by vision, and some through hearing. In behaving in this way, the subjects are showing a preference for using a particular channel, but it is not known at this time whether the preferred channel is more efficient for receiving information than is the nonpreferred channel. Such preferences occur in persons who can see well and hear well, so much more is involved than the matter of having good sense organs. The phenomenon is an interesting one, but one should not jump to the conclusion that information should be presented through both channels so that learners can use the preferred channel. It is possible that people develop preferred channels through accidents of practice. Perhaps the withdrawn bookworm learns to enjoy information presented visually, while the social success enjoys living in an auditory world. This hypothesis could be quite readily tested experimentally.

Building Visual Knowledge through Successive Sampling

In a recent study (Travers, 1969) children aged from four to twelve years were shown a picture of a common scene for 0.25 second and were asked to report what they saw. The reports showed that during this brief viewing, they picked up a very fragmentary knowledge about the picture. The children were then, once again, shown the picture and were asked to report what they saw, and so the procedure was continued for ten brief showings. The older children tended to add new items to their knowledge of the picture with each showing and sometimes corrected, later in the series, the errors made earlier. What appears to happen with these older children is that each showing gives them an opportunity to obtain a new sample of information from pictures. As the older child obtains these successive samples, he puts them together inside of himself to produce a more and more complete internal representation of the picture. The technique of showing the picture successively slows up the ordinary process of viewing a picture and extends what generally happens in a few seconds to a matter of minutes. Although the human's high-level system for processing visual information (or any other kind of information) is extremely limited in capacity, he is able to make up for this limitation by taking in successive samples of information from the picture.

There is a great amount of evidence to support a sampling theory of visual perception, which assumes that the visual perceptual system samples the vast amount of visual information available. It also seems reasonable to assume that the child has to learn to sample effectively his visual world. In the study just cited, the preschool children showed an extraordinary inability to sample the various aspects of the information in a particular picture presented to them on successive exposures. What they did was to latch onto some specific detail the first time the picture was presented and to report only that detail after each successive presentation. These young children showed an inability to slowly build up within themselves an organized conception of the picture as they examined it, and this inability seems to be attributable to an inability to sample the information present.

The results of this study fit well the results of other studies which have shown that young children in the lower elementary grades often miss items of central importance in pictures unless these items are pointed out to them. What is not known is the extent to which children can be systematically trained to sample visual information effectively so that they can build a useful conception of what they are viewing.

Signal-Noise and Signal-Signal Separation

The familiar phenomenon of the separation of the input into figure and ground—a phenomenon discussed in every textbook on perception—is discussed by physiological psychologists and engineers alike as a process of separating signal from noise. Sometimes the same problem is discussed in terms of separating one source of signals from another source of signals. In terms of the definition given here, most visual displays are not noisy, but jammed with large numbers of different sources of information. The problem of the human receiver is to separate these sources of information and to attend to that which has relevance. Such a separation is obviously of vital importance in the case of vision, since the input is rarely restricted to those visual phenomena about which information is to be transmitted.

Consider, for example, a typical sound movie used for educational purposes. The sound is likely to be limited to a single voice transmitting relevant information; on the other hand, the visual display is very rarely limited to the relevant information at hand. If, in the movie, a scientist is demonstrating an effect, the chances are that the scientist and the laboratory will appear in the picture in addition to the effect. In such a case, the images of the scientist and the laboratory represent irrelevant sources of visual information, and the effect being demonstrated represents the relevant source. The observer of the movie must discriminate and separate relevant sources from irrelevant sources. Since irrelevant sources are the overwhelmingly large part of the input of data, it is remarkable that such a separation is possible. Without such a separation, the nervous system would be flooded with irrelevant data.

There are many situations in which a similar problem exists in the auditory modality. What has been termed the "cocktail-party problem"—the separation of a voice and the message it is communicating from several simultaneous voices—is also a problem of separating signal from signal, though the problem in this case and the mechanics involved are much better understood than in the case of visual presentations.

There are obvious factors which facilitate or interfere with the separation. It is easy to attend to the louder of two voices if the contrast is great, but it not as easy to attend to the least loud. For similar reasons a whisper is difficult to separate if it is voiced against a loud, noisy background. There is not too much difficulty in accounting for the fact that a loud signal can be separated from a background of considerably *less* intense noise. Much more difficult to account for is the common situation in which several different voices are all making communications within close range of one another and in which a receiver is able to listen to and receive the message from only one source.

That different voices can be listened to even when there are many different persons speaking is a well-known fact. Such a situation can be described as one in which there are many external channels of communication operating, each one providing a high level of traffic, but in which a selection is made of the source to be attended to. Broadbent (1962) suggests that *one* basis on which voices can be discriminated is the frequency with which the voices are modulated. Two distinct voices, modulated at different frequencies, will produce a response in different regions of the basilar membrane. In such a case, the two voices would be transmitted by distinct bundles of nerve fibers. However, as the modulating frequencies approach one another, there will be an increasing overlap in the basilar-membrane fibers involved and increasing difficulty in discriminating the one message from the other.

Despite the fact that two messages transmitted simultaneously by the same voice (as when two messages are superimposed on a tape) sound like a babble, the persevering listener can, by exercising effort, discriminate and unscramble the two messages. The task does not seem to involve a peripheral mechanism; rather, it is an unscrambling undertaken centrally in the nervous system.

There is some evidence that some of the information needed for signal separation in the cocktail-party problem comes from a combination of the time difference with which the signal reaches the two ears. Two signals, one wanted and the other unwanted, are best separated by the receiver when the signals reaching the two ears arrive with the greatest time separation. A source located to the side of the head provides a signal that reaches one ear before it reaches the other, but a source in front of the person provides a signal that reaches both ears at the same time. Signal sources on opposite sides of the head provide a maximum difference in this respect and hence are most readily separated from one another. The data collected by these investigators fit the observation that persons deaf in one ear have much greater difficulty in separating two sources of verbal communication than do persons with binaural hearing. The mechanism appears to be similar to that which communication engineers refer to as *cross correlation*.

However, not all of the process of signal separation occurs through the mechanism involving time differences, for other important factors play a part. Cherry (1953) and later workers have shown that message separation is also highly dependent upon the person's knowledge of what word can be expected to follow what word in ordinary speech, that is, the transitional probabilities. Two messages consisting of meaningless strings of words are very hard to separate, but messages that have coherence can generally be separated, with the one message being fully understood and the other not acknowledged. The separation is, then, dependent upon knowledge previously acquired about the language in which the overlapping signals occur. This means that a person learns that certain words typically follow other words and that a message can be separated from other messages because the words flow in a sequence that corresponds to expectation. One suspects that on this account young children might have much greater difficulty in separating auditory communications than would adults, who have had longer experience with the use of language. Another mechanism, suggested by Broadbent (1962), is related to the fact that speakers differ in the basic speech frequency modulated by enunciation processes (that is, the pitch of the voice).

He suggests that voices and their messages can be separated through a capacity of the ear to identify basic modulation frequencies and to separate the messages which they carry from voices involving different modulation frequencies.

The mechanisms involved in the separation of signal from signal and signal from noise work sufficiently well in most human receivers that few teachers even recognize that the separation process could possibly produce problems. There are some striking cases where difficulties related to such separation play a part. For example, the typical brain-damage syndrome in a child is commonly manifested by a high degree of distractibility. Such a child seems overwhelmed when placed in a situation in which there are many different sources of information. One solution to his learning problem is to limit the number of sources by having the child alone in a simple, quiet, and rather drab room. Such a limitation of signal sources appears to improve the learning of such children. Another more common example in which children have difficulty in separating a communication from noise is found in classrooms in which there is a projector, the noise from which may well mask the audio portion of the film. The masking in such cases is particularly marked since the basic frequency of the male voice, typically used in the sound channel, is not too different from some of the predominant noise frequencies. A better separation of signal from noise might well be provided if a female voice were used.

Much less is known about the process involved in signal-signal and signal-noise separation in the case of vision than in the case of hearing. The directional nature of vision and the high information-carrying capacity of the *fovea* (central area of vision) also provide means whereby information may be obtained from certain selected aspects of the environment to the partial exclusion of others. The cues which permit the separation of visual-signal sources have not yet been identified. Furthermore, nothing is known about any learning that may be involved. It may well be that young children in the lower elementary grades have more difficulty in signal-signal separation than do older children, which suggests that there may be advantages in providing the younger children with a visually simpler environment. Unfortunately, the trend in education has been the reverse. The tendency has been to fill classrooms with numerous visual sources of information, as if the presence of these sources necessarily added to the informational intake. Much the same has been true in visual presentations by means of films. Displays on any particular frame of the film tend to be very complex. It is a rare producer who eliminates all but the essential visual features necessary for transmitting the pertinent information.

Chapter 5

The Human Information System as a Single-Channel System

One of the quite extraordinary characteristics of the human is his capacity to attend selectively to particular aspects of information in an environment that is overwhelmingly rich in information. It is this capacity that is the focus of interest of this chapter; but before exploring the topic further, we must consider the use of two terms that are widely used in related literature—often with a variety of meanings.

The first of these terms is *channel*. In the original Shannon model (1949), the word *channel* was used to describe any physical means of transmitting a message. In the case of telephonic communication, the wire is the channel. In the case of oral speech communication, the channel involves the brain of the transmitter, the nerves to the speech organs and the speech organs themselves, the air, the ear drum of the receiver, and so forth. In this meaning of the term, a part of a channel can carry several messages simultaneously. When two persons are talking simultaneously to a third person, the channel is partly shared by the two transmitters. They share the air as a channel and also the sensory-reception mechanism of the third person, who is receiving the message. Generally in psychological literature, writers refer to two messages as being transmitted by different channels even when the messages share some part of the transmitting system. For this reason, when alternate words of messages are sent into the two ears, one would say that there are two channels involved. Also, if two speakers are directing communications toward a third person, then two channels are also involved.

The term *medium* does not have any clear technical significance. It is generally used to denote a part of the communication channel that has certain physical features. Thus one speaks of the television medium or the motion-picture medium. Perhaps educational media represent little more than classes of educational materials.

The Information-Utilization Channel

In previous chapters we have touched upon the fact that as information is transmitted in the communication channel within the receiver, it is analyzed, first crudely and then at higher levels in increasingly greater detail. Up to this point we have considered those aspects of information processing that lead to the recognition of objects and events in the environment. Much of our psychological life is occupied by this kind of recognition process, which is typically a terminal process. Thus, when one walks down the street, the familiar scenes are recognized in passing, but the impression of each is readily discarded as a new, succeeding impression confronts us. The incoming information is matched with a set of expectancies, and insofar as there is a match, there is no further use for the incoming information. Much of our perception involves this kind of matching and monitoring with only the most temporary use of the information presented.

Single-Channel and Multichannel Systems in Information Processing

The reader has already been made familiar with the fact that when visual information enters the perceptual system, the different cues that it presents and that have to be identified for the input to be recognized are all identified simultaneously. This is evident from the fact that within wide limits information-processing time is independent of the number of cues that have to be analyzed in order for the information to be identified. Each cue-analysis system can be considered as a separate channel, and all of these channels operate at the same time as a series of parallel analyzer mechanisms. The operation of all of these analyzers at the same time leads to recognition. Hence one can say that up to the point of recognition in the case of the visual perceptual system, the mechanism functions as a system of parallel information channels. The reader will also recall that, in the case of the auditory system, information is received and then held in temporary storage in chunks. The chunk is then analyzed, also by the use of a series of analyzers which work in parallel. Thus the auditory system, up to the point where the input is recognized, works largely as a system of parallel channels each one of which analyzes a specific aspect of the input.

The next question that has to be considered is what happens beyond that point where information has been recognized and becomes stored in the short-term storage system and is then utilized for various purposes. The major model of the latter aspect of the information system has been developed by Broadbent (1958).

The core concept of the Broadbent model is that the information-utilization channel, which Broadbent refers to as the P-system, is a limited-capacity system that can handle only a given amount of information in a given time. The system generally handles one message at a time, and thus is referred to as a single-channel system. Through some simple and ingenious experiments Broadbent has shown that when more information arrives at the perceptual system than can be handled, some of the information is stored in a holding mechanism. In the Broadbent model, the function of the holding mechanism is to permit the take-in of larger quantities of information than the P-system can immediately handle. The holding mechanism keeps the information for a short time until the P-system is cleared and is able to handle it.

The P-system in the Broadbent model corresponds most closely in the present context with the channel involved in the utilization of information at the most detailed levels. Such utilization of information leads either to decision making or to storage in the permanent memory system. The perceptual processes that have been previously discussed, involving the low-level monitoring of incoming information, are not included in the P-system. Thus the latter system involves only a limited aspect of the total perceptual system, but it is that aspect which involves the most specific utilization of the information. In terms of the problem of constructing audiovisual materials, the kinds of information considered by the designer to be crucial are those which he hopes will enter the P-system.

When information is arriving at a slow rate through more than one of the perceptual systems, all of the information that reaches the point of recognition may enter the P-system. One can listen to a slow and dull story told on the radio at the same time that one can watch the birds on the lawn outside the window. Information from both of these sources can enter the P-system simultaneously because the two sources together provide less information than the system can handle. When the amount of information from the sources is increased, as when the story suddenly becomes interesting and begins to move at a more rapid pace, then the P-system will eventually reach the point where it cannot handle both sources. As that point is reached, the P-system will accommodate the message from only one source and exclude the messages from other sources; thus it tends to function more and more as a single-channel system.

Broadbent has proposed a mechanism to account for the selection of information for entry into the P-system. His suggestion is that between the sensory input of information and the P-system there is a *filter* which can be set to pass specific classes of information. The filter sets priorities for what will be received by the P-system. When a person is reading a book, his filter is set to pass the information derived from the pages of the book, and will pass no other information except that having very high priority. An example of such high-priority information which the filter is always set to pass is the cry "Help!"

When the P-system is operating as a single channel, the processing of information is not just limited to that derived from a single perceptual system; it is restricted even more to that derived from a single source and single channel. The tendency for the perceptual system to function as a single-channel system was noted by Cherry (1953) in demonstrations related to the cocktail-party problem. Cherry went on to demonstrate that when a person had different messages transmitted separately to the two ears and was asked to attend to and repeat one message, the content of the other message became lost. Indeed, the person involved in such an experiment might even not be able to identify the language of the message to the ear that had not been monitored.

The concept that the higher levels of the nervous system function as a single-channel conveyer of information find some support from the field of physiology in a phenomenon known as the *Hernandez-Peon effect*. There is some controversy concerning the precise explanation of the phenomenon; nevertheless, it supports the position that the higher levels of the nervous system function as a single-channel system. In the original research on the problem, electrodes were implanted in the cochlea nucleus of a cat. This nucleus is the relay point where information received by the ear is received from the auditory nerve and is then sent on to higher levels of the nervous system. When clicklike sounds are transmitted to the ear of the cat, bursts of nerve impulses can be recorded in the cochlea nucleus. In the Hernandez-Peon experiment, the cat was exposed to the clicks continuously. Significant stimuli were then introduced one at a time. One of these involved two mice in a closed bottle, another involved fish odors, and a third was an electric shock delivered to the paw.

When any one of these stimuli was introduced to the cat, the bursts of nerve impulses in the cochlea nucleus stopped. Apparently, the sound was blocked from reaching the higher centers. Hernandez-Peon interpreted his data to show that the nervous system blocked information in the auditory system when information of significance to the animal was being received by one of the other senses. Hernandez-Peon and his associates went on to show that trivial visual information tended to be blocked when significant auditory information, such as the squeak of a mouse, was being received by the cat.

Although there is some evidence that the transmission of auditory information can be blocked through electrical stimulation of certain parts of the brain of the cat, one cannot be sure that Hernandez-Peon was demonstrating such a phenomenon. There is some evidence that sensory information involving the channel receiving the trivial signal, such as the clicks, may have been blocked by the cat's turning its ears away from the source. Visual information could also be blocked by the animal's closing its eyes.

Regardless of the mechanisms involved, there is a clear tendency for an animal under experimental conditions to block in some way all trivial information and to direct its energies toward receiving the message of significance. In this respect, the animal behaves, in the presence of significant stimuli, as a single-channel system for the handling of information.

The data from such experiments must be regarded with reservation for another reason. The data are not always entirely clear, in that the electrodes implanted at some point in the nervous system pick up signals that are always contaminated with noise. For this reason it is difficult to determine whether sensory information has been entirely blocked or whether the transmission has been, in some way, reduced in intensity. The best guess at this time is that the signal is in some way weakened or attenuated since this is generally the fate of signals that are not attended to.

The Broadbent model has utility in the design of instructional devices in that it provides a simplified representation of information processing at the higher levels of the perceptual systems. The model dramatizes the difference between the task of the viewer when confronted with a mass of perceptual information which he has only to monitor, or perhaps scan to pick up particular pieces of information, and the task of making a detailed analysis of small segments of the information presented. One suspects that the presentation of audiovisual materials in schools involves more often a monitoring activity rather than an activity involving a detailed analysis of what is presented. There is a built-in temptation for the pupil to sit back and watch the movie, a task which is inherently pleasurable, rather than to undertake an analytic task, which is inherently demanding and perhaps much less pleasurable. How instructional situations have to be designed so that an analytic activity takes place rather than a passive observing one is not clear.

In the presentation of some audiovisual teaching materials, the student probably does not function as a single-channel system because the rate at which relevant information is received is probably quite slow. Only in rare instances is the rate of *relevant* information presentation so rapid that the learner might be forced to function as a single-channel system. However, there are cases where the latter might happen. For example, in a film showing heart-transplant surgery, so many events might be happening during the critical stages of the operation that the viewer might become quite oblivious of anything that the commentator might be saying. In such a presentation of surgery, as it actually occurred, there would be no good way of slowing up the presentation without losing an understanding of the timing of events, a factor critical to the success of the entire procedure. The film could be cut, and small sections could be presented one at a time, perhaps preceded by commentary, but a surgeon who wanted to see the record of the entire procedure would have to view the continuous film of the entire operation. Under the latter condition, there would be no time available for switching back and forth between the visual presentation and spoken commentary. The editor of such a film presentation should be sure that commentary is not introduced at times when it is critical that the viewer should be concentrating on the screen.

Inputs through Multiple Perceptual Systems

Now let us turn to the question of whether the input of information through two perceptual systems results in more effective learning than when only one system is used. The literature of the audiovisual field of the past has answered the question with an emphatic "Yes," on the basis of the most flimsy evidence, but the Broadbent model suggests that no advantage is to be achieved unless the capacity of the P-system is not being fully utilized. In order to obtain a clear answer, the question must first be stated with greater precision.

The question we have asked can pertain to three rather different information-reception situations. First, there is the situation in which the same information is transmitted simultaneously through two perceptual systems, as when the pupil reads directions while he hears the teacher read the same directions aloud to him. In this case, redundant information is provided through the visual and auditory perceptual systems. Second, there is the situation in which different (nonredundant) information is transmitted through two perceptual systems, as when a learner sees an English word and simultaneously hears its equivalent in a foreign language. At the beginning of the learning session, the English word and the foreign word represent nonredundant information to the learner. Thus, the first two of these conditions differ in the extent to which they involve the transmission of redundant information. A third condition is rather different, for it involves the alternate use of one perceptual system and then another, as when a person first hears a speech and then reads a mimeographed version of it, or when a student of Russian first reads a sentence in Russian and then hears the same sentence spoken. The question in this third case is whether it is more efficient to present the same material twice through the same perceptual system or to alternate perceptual systems. Let us consider each of these three conditions of multiple inputs.

First, there is the situation in which identical information is transmitted simultaneously through two perceptual systems. This is the classic case described in audiovisual textbooks which all cite the same studies to support the contention that more efficient learning is achieved through the simultaneous presentation of the same information through two perceptual systems than through one. Unfortunately, most of these studies were conducted long before behavioral scientists had learned to exercise proper caution in the design of experiments and before statistical tests of significance had become mandatory. Although the studies did show some tendency for the multiperceptual-system presentations to produce more effective transmissions of information than were provided by the single transmissions, the differences were probably not large enough to be either significant or consequential. The Broadbent model leads one to expect that the transmission of redundant information through two perceptual systems will not lead to more effective information transmission than the use of a single modality except when the rate of information transmission is very slow. With this hypothesis in mind, Van Mondfrans and Travers (1965) conducted a carefully designed experiment in which information was transmitted through the eye and the ear simultaneously, through the eye alone, and through the ear alone. No evidence could be found for any superiority of the information transmission through two inputs over one. With the young adult, the eye-alone situation was as effective as the ear and the eye together. As is typical in research with nonsense syllables, the ear alone generally resulted in inferior performance to the eye-alone situation.

The data from the Van Mondfrans and Travers experiment fitted the research-derived model of Broadbent, but ran contrary to the model of multisensory learning presented in textbooks in the audio-visual field. It is quite evident that the audiovisual model of the past is fundamentally unsound and must be discarded.

The second learning situation considered is one in which non-redundant information is transmitted through two different perceptual systems, as when the auditory channel provides information different from that transmitted by the visual channel. Some research has been done on this problem. In addition, some earlier data originally col-lected for a different purpose has been reworked (see Travers, 1967). The findings are clear. The two channels together do not result in the retention of greater quantities of information than when one channel is used alone. Block one channel and more is learned through the remaining channel, but the gain and the loss are about equal. The data generally suggest that the main factor limiting the rate at which information is received and at least temporarily stored depends on events at the highest levels of the nervous system and not on the number of perceptual systems through which information is transmitted. In the bisensory condition (Travers, Chan & Van Mond-frans, 1965), it has been found that adding color and embellishment to the visual channel increased information acquisition through that channel, but the gain is accompanied by a corresponding loss of information acquired through the auditory channel. The data are always as though the senses were pumping information into a single narrow and limited-capacity system that could handle only so much information and no more.

A situation still more complicated than any considered here, but involving the simultaneous transmission of nonredundant information through two different perceptual systems also needs to be considered. It is that in which the information in the auditory channel is used to cue perceptual processes in the visual channel. Thus the sound track of a motion picture may say, "Look at the red circular object in the middle of the picture." Such a cue probably presents no perceptual problems since the verbal commentary is typically given at such a slow rate that it is unlikely to occupy fully the information channel and, hence, sufficient information capacity is left for the examination of the red object. Of course, if much commentary is to be given, then a more efficient communication can be made by presenting the material in printed form rather than orally, except when the audiences are very young.

Now let us turn to the third condition in which the perceptual channel is alternated, as when vision is first used, then hearing, then vision, and so on. At least two factors have to be considered in determining the effect on learning of such switching. First, there is the matter of whether there is a loss of time involved in switching. Second, there is the possibility, raised by Broadbent, that after one perceptual system has been used for a time, other perceptual systems acquire a heightened readiness to receive information. These two factors appear to operate in opposite directions to one another; one suggests that switching perceptual systems involves loss of time, while the other implies an advantage in switching. Some experimental evidence throws light on the first factor, time loss.

Reid and Travers (1968) reported a study in which subjects learned nonsense syllables, but under conditions that involved the switching of perceptual systems. Under the condition with maximum switching, the ten nonsense syllables to be learned were presented alternately through the eye and the ear. In such a case, 10 trials with the syllables involved 90 switches. The results from learning under the latter condition could then be compared with the learning of two groups, one of which learned the syllables through an auditory presentation and one through a visual presentation. The condition requiring a switching of perceptual channels resulted in a decrement in learning of about 15 per cent as compared with the conditions under which no switching was required. From the data, a computation could be made of the time lost in switching. This was computed to be approximately one-fifth of a second per switch, a result that agrees well with that derived from other estimates. There is also some evidence that switching from perceptual system to perceptual system involves about the same time loss as switching from one message source to another.

One can predict with some certainty that most tasks involving the use of audiovisual materials would not involve a comparable amount of loss resulting from the need to shift from one input to another. First, the number of switches involved is likely to be quite small. Second, the loss in time resulting from switching probably occurs only when the information that is being used by the learner is less than that which the higher levels of the system can handle. Thus one might expect to find that the loss due to switching is probably quite small in the use of most audiovisual devices.

The second phenomenon related to switching, one that supposedly provides an advantage, needs to be explored experimentally. One can well assume that any advantage would be most evident in tasks that were long and tedious. Perhaps a long and dull book might be easier to study if two versions were available, one in the usual printed form and the other in the form of rapid, compressed speech. The student could then alternate the use of the two forms of the material and perhaps break some of the monotony involved in study. The main reason that this method has not been studied is that the tasks involved would have to be extremely long and would involve very large amounts of time on the part of the learner.

Finally, the point must be made that rapid channel switching back and forth represents a highly novel situation not ordinarily encountered in daily life. There is a possibility that an increase in speed of switching might occur if a person were given practice at engaging in this kind of activity. The switching that occurs at a cocktail party, as one first monitors a snatch of one conversation and then a snatch of another, is a leisurely kind of switching compared with that required in the Reid and Travers experiment in which switching occurred once every second. The area is full of research problems that need to be studied.

Inputs through more than one perceptual system serve another rather interesting, but ill-understood function. A child who is shown some unusual object is not content to just look at it. The chances are that he will want to touch and handle it and, if very young, may attempt to explore it with his mouth and tongue. The human never completely loses this kind of exploratory tendency. Department stores display signs warning that the customer handles merchandise at his own risk, because customers are not content to look but have a compulsion to pick up objects and explore them with their haptic perceptual system. In the case of the adult in the department store, the exploration of objects by touch and movement is generally quite unnecessary for deciding whether or not to make a purchase, but seems to be undertaken for the satisfaction that such exploration brings. Why this kind of multisensory exploration occurs at all is very puzzling and open to conjecture. Cautious exploration does have survival value, but the puzzling point is why it tends to be undertaken through a multisensory approach. One can well suspect that man prefers to form concepts of objects that include multiple sources of information derived from different perceptual systems than concepts derived from a single system, but this kind of statement explains nothing. Certainly, every kindergarten teacher assumes that a child prefers to have a concept of a sheep which includes not only the visible appearance of the sheep but also the sound it makes. Perhaps, on this account, audiovisual materials must be inevitable sources of frustration to the young, who have an inner urge to touch as well as to hear and to see. Still, seeing and hearing together is probably less frustrating than seeing alone or hearing alone.

Before leaving the problem of multichannel inputs, we should note a gross procedural error which has produced misleading conclusions from many studies in this area, including some quite recent studies. Let us consider this error by way of an example. Suppose that a study were conducted in which verbal material was learned by being presented through the auditory channel, through the visual channel, or through both channels at the same time. The findings were that, on the average, 20 units were learned when the auditory channel was used, 30 units when the visual channel was used, and 30 channels when both channels were used. Now, the author of such a study might do what investigators have misleadingly done in the past. He might average the learning occurring under the two single-channel conditions, arriving at an average of 25 units learned, and then compare this figure with the average learning under the two-channel condition, namely 30 units. This would lead him to the thoroughly false conclusion that learning under the single-channel condition is less efficient than learning under the multichannel condition. Such a conclusion has often been erroneously drawn from these kinds of data in this kind of way. The correct conclusion is that the multi-channel condition and the visual condition provide similar amounts of learning, but that the auditory channel leads to less learning. In such studies the auditory channel generally produces less learning because spoken words are more ambiguous than printed words.

Unfortunately, erroneously drawn conclusions of this kind are often widely quoted in textbooks in the audiovisual field, before the basic fallacy underlying them is revealed.

Some Characteristics of Visual and Auditory Information in Educational Settings

There are not too many situations in which the same information is presented through the eye and the ear. Indeed, the case of perfect parallelism between print and speech is almost unique. The two sets of symbols show a close correspondence and provide almost parallel meanings. This kind of parallelism of information supplied through the auditory and visual channels is used in educational settings only in the administration of tests, where the long-established practice has been to read the directions to the person taking the test while he reads them himself from the printed copy. The latter procedure has been established by custom and not on the basis of empirical research or theory. The more usual state of affairs is for the auditory channel to be filled with symbolic material, either speech or music, and the visual channel to present noncoded materials from the natural world. In such a situation, learning often involves the acquisition of vocabulary representing objects in the real world. The sound track teaches the symbolic equivalents of objects and events in the real world. A film showing an amoeba wriggling around in a drop of water is likely to be accompanied by a statement that the animal is an amoeba, that the dark portion of the body of the animal is the nucleus, that the light areas within the body of the organism are vacuoles, and so forth. The auditory channel provides information that makes it ultimately possible for the student to think about the amoeba in precise terms without the actual presence of the organism. When the film is first run, the information in the two channels is nonredundant. One of the tasks of the student in learning from the film is to tie together the symbolic material in the auditory channel with the objects and events of the real world presented through the visual channel.

The auditory channel is thoroughly accepted by most people as the channel for symbolic and abstract communications, and the visual channel is taken for granted as the channel through which direct information about the world of real events is received. Probably for this reason, when abstract material is presented through the visual system, as it is when abstract art is viewed, there is a marked tendency for viewers to reject such material. A common remark of a person viewing a painting of the modern school is, "If I knew what the picture meant, I might like it." Yet nobody ever asks what Beethoven's *Fifth Symphony* means. The listener takes for granted that music does not have to "mean" anything. The reverse is also true. When a piece of music is designed to represent some event in the real world, such as a kitten scampering over the keys of the piano, it is treated as an oddity or perhaps even as a piece which does not represent respectable music.

The cross-coding of the real world with the world of symbols is one of the more important functions performed by audiovisual materials. In the learning of the verbal code that corresponds to real events, there are advantages, as Mueller and Travers (1965) have shown, in presenting simultaneously the two items to be associated together. If this is done, there should be a brief pause of at least a few seconds, before the next item of information is transmitted. The pause is necessary in order to provide the time needed for the learner to hook up the two items. The continuous flow of sound and picture is not an appropriate technique to use when word-object associations are to be learned.

This does not mean that under all conditions the simultaneous presentation of the visual material and the auditory-verbal material is desirable. One could certainly imagine complex visual presentations which might so fully occupy the perceptual system of the viewer that any additional auditory information would be blocked. A film designed to familiarize the viewer with a complex piece of machinery might well allow the viewer time to view the entire machine, as a whole and from different angles, while the sound track is left empty. As some perceptual familiarity with the equipment is achieved, then explanatory materials can be introduced.

Brief mention must also be made of the case where objects from the real world are used as symbols, as when a stone arch is used to represent a human organization and the narrator makes the point that when all the stones are in their proper place, the arch is a strong structure. Where analogies of this kind are used, the learner has to be instructed in the meaning of the symbolism involved. What this means is that a part of the learning time is used for learning a symbolic system, and this time has to be taken out of the time used for learning. Such use of nonconventional systems of symbols is of doubtful instructional value since the audience is required to learn a symbol system that will not be encountered again. A learning situation should never involve the acquisition of skills that have no future utility.

The Affect That Surrounds Perceptions

The information received about the environment is always colored by what psychologists call *affect,* that is, by the experience of being pleased, or repulsed, or bored, or anxious, or otherwise moved. When someone enters the room, we do not see just a person; we may see a threatening person, but our secretary (who also sees him) describes him as a distinguished person. Perception always involves a great amount of color, or affect, that often leads to misinterpretation. The source is complex and is far from being completely understood, but there is some agreement that it is intimately associated with inputs to the central nervous system from sense organs that lie deep within the muscles, joints, viscera, and other organs.

The point has already been made that the receptor system includes sense organs embedded deeply within the body that provide important information concerning bodily states. Receptors within the muscles, for example, provide information pertaining to tension within the muscles or pressure on the muscles from the outside. When muscles are in a state of tension, volleys of impulses are transmitted through sensory pathways to the central nervous system. The volleys may be of such a magnitude that they provide an unpleasant experience. Indeed, extreme muscular tension may produce an experience described as painful. Additional inputs also come from the viscera, and these are likely to be particularly pronounced during what are described as emotional states. The inputs of the sensory system derived from the viscera have their own particular quality in experience and, in extreme form, are often described as "sickening" sensations. The inputs giving information about conditions within the body carry with them strong affect; that is, they provide strong feeling tones that provide a background for other experiences and often color them.

The relationship of visceral sensations to sensory inputs from outside the body is complex. Suppose that a child playing near a pool of water falls in and, after struggling to avoid drowning, is rescued in a semiconscious condition. During the incident, the child experiences the terrors of a desperate person struggling to survive and also the pain that accompanies suffocation. The terror and pain have produced profound emotional responses including visceral responses which, in turn, resulted in the higher centers of the nervous system being bombarded with sensory inputs from inside the body. At the same time, something else very important happened. The visceral and other emotional responses have become classically conditioned to the stimuli provided by the swimming pool. This means that when the same child later encounters a swimming pool, even though he is a safe distance from the water, he will experience to some degree the same emotional responses that he experienced at the time when he was drowning. Indeed, the pool may fill him with much of the terror triggered by the original situation. This emotional response forms a backdrop against which he sees the pool and responds to the pool. The pool is no longer either a neutral object in terms of the value placed on it or an object which, through other associations, is regarded as pleasure-giving, but it appears as a highly aversive object likely to produce withdrawal and avoidance behaviors. Sensory inputs from inside his body fuse inextricably with the sensory inputs that come from the outside world and together form the basis for his perception of the pool.

An important point to note is that the later emotional responses that occur when the child sees the pool are classic conditioned responses. The responses were learned in the dramatic situation where the perception of the pool was accompanied by emotional responses that became conditioned to the sight of the pool. Overwhelming evidence indicates that emotional responses are readily conditioned to new stimuli in this way and, as the child grows, he acquires numerous conditioned responses of this kind so that, by the time he reaches adulthood, his perception of the outside world becomes highly colored by irrelevant emotional responses.

Sometimes, the sensory inputs from the emotional responses may be so intense that they overwhelm the inputs of information from the outside world. Experiments on the validity of the reports of those who witnessed dramatic incidents testify to the fact that emotionally derived input may overwhelm the data from the outside world. Such witnesses often fail to report correctly even the gross details of what happened, let alone the fine details.

Thus one is forced to the conclusion that man is not well built for receiving and interpreting objectively pure information from the outside world. At first sight this may seem to give man a biological disadvantage in mastering his environment and, in a civilized and protective society, it probably is a disadvantage. On the other hand, in a primitive society, the emotional responses that accompany perception may help to trigger and enhance avoidance behavior and, hence, promote survival.

What has just been said is a gross oversimplification of the coloring of the perception of the outside world by irrelevant features of the perception process. The emotional and affective attributes of all experience also derive their peculiar qualities from activities within the brain itself. There is considerable evidence that the stimulation of some centers in the limbic system of the brain provide responses similar to those that are ordinarily aroused by activities described as pleasurable. Animals will press buttons to obtain such stimulation and, even when hungry, will prefer to press such buttons than to press one that will deliver food. Pleasure, and affective responses in general, may depend at least sometimes upon the direct activation of specific centers in the brain. Without the operation of such centers, one would have difficulty in understanding the highly pleasurable responses which children manifest when confronted with bright colors. Some activity in the cortical and subcortical regions may in itself contribute substantially to the affective aspects of perception, without the intervention of diffuse emotional responses.

Chapter 6

The Role of Attention in the Human Information System

The attending response is complicated both psychologically and physiologically. The physiological aspects have been investigated mainly by Russian scientists who followed Pavlov's lead in his descriptions of what he called the *investigatory response,* a complex set of behaviors that are seen to occur when an animal is faced with a novel state of affairs in its environment. This investigatory response, today called the *orienting response,* would be widely referred to by American psychologists as an *attending response*. It also has to be distinguished from a closely related complex of behaviors known as the *startle response.*

The orienting response has many characteristic physiological features, including dilation of the pupils of the eyes and an increased sensitivity of the retina to light. Generally, it involves a movement of the body so that the sense organs have maximum opportunity for taking in information from the object in the environment that has initiated the response. The muscles tend to show some tension. Alpha waves in the brain typically disappear. Blood vessels in the head dilate. Breathing is sometimes temporarily arrested. Numerous other responses have also commonly been recorded.

The term *attention* has had a long history in psychology, and despite an extensive literature devoted to the topic, there is no clear-cut single phenomenon to which the term is widely applied. First, it is commonly used to refer to adjustments in the sensory system that facilitate the reception of particular conglomerates of information and, second, it is also used to refer to the inhibition of the reception of particular classes of information so that other classes can be more readily received. Thus, attention includes both facilitative and inhibitory factors and represents a collection of conditions that improve or depress the reception of particular items of information. A third factor involved in attention is the level of wakefulness, or arousal, of the attending person. A sleeping person does not attend to anything

115

outside of himself. A fourth factor, more appropriately described as a set of factors, relates to the conditions in the environment which favor or interfere with the reception of information.

Facilitative Factors in Attention

Emphasis has already been placed on the fact that the perceptual systems are active searching systems capable of scanning the environment for particular sources of information. Searching for information is an activity in which all higher organisms engage and which results in most of the important information that ever becomes permanently stored.

Perceptual inputs are searched for because prior learning has developed what Miller and his associates (1960) refer to as a *plan.* Without such a plan there cannot be selectivity except insofar as there are genetically established mechanisms for selecting inputs by the perceptual system. The "plan" can be considered as a system of expectancies that guide those aspects of the perceptual systems that permit input selection, but guidance is of a very general nature. During the viewing of any particular display of visual information, a somewhat different basis for the selection of what is to be attended to takes place. Hake and his associates (1966) have suggested that one important basis for the selection of what is attended to is whether it is a signal rather than noise. Thus in a photograph of a group of people, the background is indistinct and represents a display approximating visual noise. On the other hand, the individuals on whom the camera is focused represent a system of well-defined contours, and hence an information system. The fovea of the eye tends to be directed toward the people, rather than the "noisy" background.

Evidence to support this position is found in an article by Mackworth and Morandi (1967), who gave subjects various photographs to study while the movements of the eye were recorded by an eye camera. In the example illustrated in the article, the subject viewed a picture taken by astronauts of the Baja California peninsula. Subjects tended to spend most of their time examining the boundary of the peninsula at the places where the coastline was most jagged and, hence, provided the most complex display of information. The eyes spent little time directed toward the blotchy interior, where dark and shade seemed to form little more than a random pattern, or toward the smooth parts of the coastline which also provided little information. The authors of the article suggest that peripheral vision "edited out" those parts of the photograph that carried little information.

Much of the behavior that falls in the category of attention involves orienting responses and behaviors that involve searching and scanning. Skill in performing tasks involving such behavior represents an objective that schools generally seek to achieve. High-school pupils are expected to be able to scan through the pages of a book in order to locate particular items of information for writing a paper. They are also expected to be able to scan through a bibliography in order to locate items that fall into a special category. Tasks of this kind are referred to as *visual search,* or visual scanning tasks, and have been extensively studied by psychologists interested in the perceptual aspects of learning. The items searched for are commonly referred to as *targets.* The material in which the targets are embedded is said to consist of *nontarget items.* Research in this area has been opened up mainly by Neisser, much of whose work has been summarized in a single article (1964). Of considerable importance to the educator is the finding that practice produces considerable increases in skill in visual-search tasks. In these studies, as in many others in the perceptual area, the effective use of sensory information requires extended practice of a kind that is not provided by ordinary daily life. The implication is that, unless the schools provide opportunities for students to undertake visual-search tasks, little skill is likely to be acquired.

A second finding of considerable interest is that the *efficiency* of visual search can be improved by searching for more than one category at the same time. Neisser reports that, after practice, subjects were able to scan for 10 different targets as rapidly as they could scan for a single target. In searching the literature, before writing this chapter, the author scanned certain journals and articles for the several categories of information covered in this chapter. All categories were searched for at the same time. The latter procedure is more efficient than that of scanning the literature separately for each category. Just how many categories can be kept in mind by highly trained subjects without a decrement in performance is not known, but it is probably large. Neisser points out that newspaper-scanning agencies employ persons who are capable of scanning newspapers and identifying material in any of a very large number of categories. On such visual-search tasks, newsprint may be scanned at a rate of 1,000 words per minute.

Research on visual scanning has involved such tasks as the search for particular letters among series of letters or the search for particular patterns among sequences of varied patterns. Gibson and Yonas (1966), using such a task, compared the performance of second-, fourth-, and sixth-graders and college sophomores and found a steady increase in the skill with age, as one would expect. These researchers also found some results of theoretical interest. Even for these young children, searching for two target letters at the same time was no more difficult than searching for one—a result consistent with the findings of Neisser.

Some visual-scanning tasks have used materials of greater complexity. Strongman and Brown (1966) used as nontarget items three-letter nonsense syllables that could be classified with respect to high and low meaningfulness (association value) and also words of high and low frequency of occurrence. Both meaningfulness and frequency of occurrence were found to influence the degree to which target items could be readily located. In addition, the study showed that the characteristics of the context items were also important in establishing search times. Neisser, in addition to using strings of letters and digits, also used words; but no study could be found in which words had to be located in connected prose. The latter kind of situation is not one which provides a very satisfactory experimental situation, although it does have the advantage of studying the phenomenon in a context close to the form in which it is observed in an educational context.

No particularly useful model representing visual-scanning operations has been developed, but a research study by Rabbitt (1964) provides some useful cues. He presented subjects with a search task in which they had to identify certain symbols. After the subjects had practiced this task, the nontarget symbols were switched, and the switching had an adverse effect on performance. If learning the task involved only learning to identify the target symbols, a change in the nontarget symbol should have had no effect on performance. The fact that it did depress performance suggests that in a scanning task the nontarget symbols are examined, though perhaps not with the same degree of information intake as the target symbols. It is as if all symbols are crudely examined, but only those to be positively identified pass a perceptual filter. This conclusion fits the model of perception presented in this book, in which much of the perceptual input is analyzed at a low level of detail and a little of the input is analyzed in great detail.

A study by Bower (1965) led him to the conclusion that on a search task, a filter theory fits the data; that is, a scanning task can be likened to the process of setting a filter which will permit the passage of only certain items of information while all other material is blocked from entering the perceptual system. However, not only Neisser but also Strongman and Brown have provided evidence indicating that both the target and the nontarget items are examined in the scanning process, since changing the nontarget items may materially alter the difficulty of a scanning task. Such data indicate that more than a simple filter mechanism must be involved.

The area raises interesting problems for further study, many of them pertinent to problems of teaching. For example, in scanning a book for information related to a particular topic, does the efficient scanner sample the material to be covered, or is there a very rapid scanning on a word-by-word basis? Some teachers of rapid reading assume that the latter procedure is followed. There is also the possibility that efficient scanning may call for the organization of material into larger units than words.

Inhibitory Factors in Attention

Inhibitory factors in attention have only recently been brought into prominence through developments in neurophysiology. The picture of the nervous system that emerges includes the possibility that information entering through the afferent system may be blocked at a number of different points. There seems to be some possibility that the information can be blocked, or at least attenuated, at the sense-organ level. In addition, there are a number of relay points within the nervous system where a similar blocking or attenuation can take place. The inhibitory effects do not originate at the place where the inhibition takes place, but in the cerebral cortex. They represent the means whereby control is exercised over the amount and kind of information reaching the higher centers, permitting information with greater relevance to be received and information of least probable significance to have a reduced impact or, sometimes, no impact. The mechanism for the regulation of sensory inputs involves tracts that carry impulses down from the cortex to the various positions in the sensory tracts where blocking can occur.

There is another condition under which the inhibition of attention to particular stimuli appears to take place. This is the phenomenon found in vigilance studies. In this type of study, subjects are required to be attentive for a low-level signal that occurs rather rarely. In one such vigilance task, subjects were required to watch the second hand of a clock that ticked off the seconds except that, on certain occasions, the hand ticked off a two-second interval rather than the usual one second. Subjects were required to report whenever such an irregularity occurred. In other studies, subjects have had to detect the appearance of a faint auditory signal, such as a slight, momentary change in pitch in a continuous tone. There are numerous variations in such tasks.

A particularly significant aspect of behavior in such tasks is that the efficiency of the subject shows a rapid decline during the first thirty minutes of his performance. Although he may detect without error the first few signals, the number that he misses steadily increases until it reaches a steady level about half an hour after the task was begun. However, there is another aspect of this phenomenon that is particularly interesting. Broadbent (1963) has shown that the decrement does not take place if subjects are asked to report signals *even if they are not sure*. The data show that the decrement is primarily in the sureness with which the person is able to detect signals and not in the detection of signals itself. What appears to happen on such a dull, routine task is that the detection of signals at the higher levels of the nervous system becomes inhibited, but that signal detection still takes place at lower levels where a crude analysis of incoming information takes place. The higher levels of the nervous system do not permit themselves to be occupied for long with routine, repetitive tasks.

Thus inputs of sensory information are blocked under a wide range of conditions. Blocking of an input may occur because another input has priority over it. Blocking may also occur because the input of information through one perceptual system occurs infrequently. The control of attention by controlling the input is the matter now to be considered.

Novelty, Exploratory Behavior, and Attention

Psychologists have long devoted research to the study of exploratory behavior and the related problem of the effect of novelty on attention. An excellent summary of the basic research studies in this area has been provided by Berlyne (1960) and more recently by Fowler (1965).

During the past twenty-five years a great number of different experiments have appeared in which animals have been free to explore a particular environment and an attempt has been made to identify the factors that influence the amount of exploration. The environments used in such studies have been quite simple ones, often no more complicated than a large, flat area surrounded by walls which prevent the animal from escaping. Such an open area is generally marked off in squares, and the experimenter counts the number of squares that the animal enters, thereby obtaining a measure of the amount of exploration. The open area may have some barriers introduced, or it may be divided up to form a conventional maze. The subjects used in such studies vary in complexity from the cockroach to man—and with surprisingly uniform results.

A common finding in all species studied is that the amount of exploratory behavior is related to the extent to which the animal has been confined just prior to being given the opportunity to explore. A rat confined to a box that limits behavior shows more exploratory behavior on being released than one which has not been so confined. The length of confinement is also related to the amount of exploratory behavior. One is tempted to jump to the conclusion that confinement merely develops a need to exercise the muscles, but this is not so. Animals confined in large, dark boxes that permit movement also show a heightened tendency to explore when released into a lighted, open situation. A related finding is that dogs raised in a highly uniform and nonstimulating environment during the first six months of life show a much larger amount of exploratory behavior than those that have been raised in an environment filled with a rich variety of objects and events. However, this may be a different phenomenon, in that the dogs raised in a rich environment have learned to discriminate what events lead to reinforcement and what do not and, hence, restrict attention to only limited aspects of their environment.

Although there may be questions about how to interpret particular findings of particular studies, the outcomes of research generally suggest that organisms have a need to vary the sensory input and that what is called exploratory behavior does produce that kind of variation. Another kind of study also lends support to this hypothesis. This is the kind of study in which rats are placed in a T-maze—a maze that has a straight starting alley down which the rat may move until it comes to the cross piece, where it has to choose between a left turn and a right turn. In the studies under consideration, a rat is allowed to move down the straight alley of the T-maze and, at the choice point, makes either a right or a left turn. Then the animal is placed back in the starting position, and one of the branches of the T is changed, generally by changing the walls from a plain, uniform gray to a black-and-white pattern. On the second trial, the animal shows a tendency to choose the alley that has had a change made in the walls. If no change is made, then it tends to choose the alley that it did *not* enter on the previous occasion.

Just as hungry animals can learn to perform various skills through appropriate reinforcement with food, so too animals can learn when the only reinforcement is that of having access to spaces to be explored. A variety of animals have learned to run mazes when the only "reward" at the goal was that of spending time in an open space.

The seeking out of new perceptual inputs seems to be a crucial factor in exploratory behavior and is particularly well brought out in those studies that have investigated the effect of novel objects on behavior. In such studies a novel object is any object that has not been present previously in the animal's environment.

A great many different species have shown a tendency to orient themselves toward novel objects. Some animals, typically from the domestic species, show strong tendencies to manifest approach behavior toward novel objects. Other animals show watchful attentiveness, but no approach. While the laboratory rat will approach and explore a novel object, the wild Norwegian rat will watch, but will not approach anything strange. Indeed, the wild strain will almost die from starvation before it will venture to taste some unusual food. Such caution and fearfulness perhaps account for the fact that the wild rat is the only creature that has successfully competed with man for survival.

Novelty effects show satiation. An animal will show approach behavior toward a novel object and examine it, but the object rapidly loses drawing power. What is not known is the extent to which satiation with one novel object produces satiation for all novel objects. If a child is given several novel objects to examine and play with in succession, does he then begin to tire of all further novel objects? The answer to such a question is quite crucial for the design of educational materials. The designers of audiovisual materials give the impression of assuming that the child has an insatiable appetite for the novel, but perhaps there are times in an educational program when a dull and boring task may serve the purpose of building up an appetite for the novel.

Just as animals will learn when the only reinforcement is the opportunity to explore, so too will they learn when the only reinforcement is the opportunity to be attentive to or to manipulate some novel object. The evidence suggests that the phenomenon involves a strong and basic tendency in living things. Such a tendency obviously has survival value in most species. Creatures that do not quickly attend to the novel in their environment would be rapidly exterminated for, in the wild state, the novel is typically threatening rather than benevolent. In addition, exploratory tendencies have value in searching for food. An animal that beats the same path each day would rapidly run out of sources of food.

One should show some caution in the application of research on exploration and curiosity to the design of audiovisual materials. The results show how deprivation from novelty and novelty itself can be used to control attention, but attention to an object is no guarantee that information about that object will be stored in permanent memory. Attention can be considered to be a necessary but not a sufficient condition for the efficient intake of information. The design of a teaching device that ensures attention and nothing else is not a good design. Indeed, many motion pictures can be criticized on the basis that they employ attention-getting devices that do not teach.

Reward and Punishment in Relation to Attention

The relationship of reward and punishment to attention is complex. This problem has been studied within a number of different experimental contexts. One approach has been to determine whether objects associated with reward tend to be fixated by the eyes in preference to objects that have not been associated with reward. Another approach is to present subjects with ambiguous figures (figures which can be seen in two different ways) and to reward the subject for seeing the figure in one way and, perhaps, punish him for seeing it in the other way. Under such circumstances, does the subject tend to see it more and more in the rewarded way? A third approach is to study the effects of punishment and reward on the detection of very faint signals and to ask whether these conditions facilitate detection. A great many techniques have evolved for the study of this problem.

In the case of reward, the results are fairly clear-cut. If an object is associated with reward, then it is more likely to be attended to than an object not associated with reward. The next question that one may ask is whether the effect of reward on attention is greater or less than the effect of punishment, but this question is not readily answered. On the one hand, the answer is likely to depend on the amount of the reward and the amount of punishment, but reward and punishment cannot be measured in comparable terms. On the other hand, experiments on the effect of punishment on attention often appeared to have inconsistent effects which long puzzled research workers. However, this apparent inconsistency has been resolved independently by Berlyne (1960) and Solley and Murphy (1960). These investigators note that experiments involving attention and perception have used punishment under two different kinds of conditions. In some experiments, the subject has been punished whenever a particular object has been presented; he cannot escape punishment. In other experiments, the appearance of the stimulus signaling punishment is also a signal for the subject to take some action that will prevent the punishment from taking place. The results of these two groups of experiments show a fairly clear and consistent picture. If a stimulus is a signal for unavoidable punishment, then sensitivity to the signal and attention to it are likely to be depressed. If, in contrast, the stimulus signals that punishment will follow unless the individual takes some action, then sensitivity to the stimulus is enhanced. Thus, in the one case involving sure punishment, the stimulus tends to be ignored; but in the other case, more carefully directed attention results.

There is no problem is obtaining the attention of students to most audiovisual materials, partly because, in terms of our analysis here, watching television and listening to radio have been rewarding experiences. The tendency to attend is then carried over to the related situations in school of watching a display on a screen or listening to a tape recording. This carryover often provides the illusion that these devices are promoting learning, in that an observer can fail to recognize that watching is not the equivalent of learning. In addition, the point must be made that in watching a television screen or a screen on which a motion picture is being shown in a semidarkened room, the observer tends to maintain a posture of watchfulness because the optical device has certain features working for it. One feature is that it presents moving images, and the visual system gives priority to anything that moves. Another feature is the fact that the images on the screen have an intensity greater than that of the objects in the room. Once again, the image on the screen has a characteristic which gives it a priority of entry into the perceptual system.

A fairly strong case can be made that displays which produce what psychologists call *positive affect* (and what the layman calls *pleasure*) tend to be more readily attended to and to be regarded longer than neutral displays. Brown and Farha (1966) showed that merely giving subjects an expectancy that attending to a display would be pleasant increased the viewing time. These same investigators also showed that displays covering a larger area tended to be viewed longer than smaller displays. For reasons that are not fully understood, the large-screen presentation would appear to have pleasure value and attention-attracting value that the small screen does not have.

Incidental Learning

Some information of considerable interest related to the problems we are considering has come from an area of research on *incidental learning*. The research designs follow a common pattern. A subject is given a task to perform, such as learning nonsense syllables, which is designated as the main task. As he performs this learning task, he also learns information about aspects of the situation which he was not required to learn. He may, for example, learn the color in which each nonsense syllable is printed. Learning of the latter kind is referred to as incidental learning, and the tasks thus performed are sometimes referred to as subsidiary, or incidental, tasks to distinguish them from the main task.

An especially interesting finding is that the more a person is motivated to perform the main task, the less he learns from the subsidiary tasks. Attention may vary in the extent to which it is diffuse or concentrated; that is, the learner varies in the extent to which he takes in broad features of a situation or very narrow and limited features. One probably should assume that the capacity of the higher centers for handling information does not become greater when attention is diffuse. Under the diffuse condition a greater range of events in the environment may be observed than under the concentrated condition, but one must assume that this also takes more time or that the events are scanned at a less detailed level. It seems very unlikely that diffuse attention will result in the taking in of more information per unit of time than concentrated attention.

Environmental Complexity and Attention

As with much of the other knowledge in the area of attention, research on the effect of complexity in the environment has been undertaken with a number of different species and with remarkably uniform results. Rats placed in a maze and given the choice of entering an alley painted a uniform gray and an alley painted with a design show a preference for the alley with the design. Very young children show a related phenomenon. Thomas (1965) showed that infants aged between 2 and 14 weeks tended to avoid fixating the simplest of a number of designs. The technique involved observing the direction of gaze of the infants as they lay on their backs and recording the time spent fixating each of three displays. One of the two more complex of the displays resembled a human face, but the infants showed no particular preference for fixating that particular design. The phenomenon shown in the Thomas study of subjects preferring the more complex of designs has also been demonstrated with older children and with adults.

There is also some evidence suggesting that there may be an optimum level of complexity of a display for holding attention. Vitz (1966) found some evidence to support this hypothesis which makes a great deal of sense. Very simple displays contain so little information that the subject becomes rapidly inhibited with respect to observing them. The more complex displays may be so difficult to structure that they communicate no information at all and are responded to as though they contained very little information.

These findings fit the model of behavior proposed by Fowler (1965) which has as its central proposition that organisms need, seek, and process information. The tendency to attend to a particular display appears to depend upon the amount of information that the display can provide.

The factor of complexity certainly should be considered in the design of audiovisual materials, though guidelines can hardly be set at this time. One can guess that materials are much more likely to err on the side of being too complex than on the side of being too simple, particularly in view of the predilection of some movie directors for embellishment and for communication by innuendo. The phenomenon that is to be attended to is generally of a sufficient degree of complexity to assure attention without adding a complex setting.

The Energizing Effect of Sensory Stimulation

There can be little doubt that a necessary condition for learning is wakefulness and that wakefulness can vary from deep coma to a condition of hyperexcitability. There is also evidence that massive sensory inputs energize behavior. This fact is obvious from daily experience. The loud nightclub band excites the guests who have been conditioned to sleep at that particular hour. The noise of crude instruments, together with much shouting, is used to work up primitive people into a frenzy at their tribal gatherings. The roar of Niagara arouses deep emotion in those who take the trip beneath the Falls. Sensory inputs do far more than provide the individual with information about his environment. They also have the effect of raising the level of activity in the nervous system. The designer of audiovisual materials is not unaware of the activating effect that sound and vision may sometimes produce; loud music, intense sounds, and dramatic lighting effects seem to be introduced for the sole purpose of arousing the student from a state of lethargy. Such attempts to produce arousal must be distinguished from attempts to produce interest. The one has to do with raising the level of excitement, the other pertains to the extent to which the individual prefers and seeks certain classes of information rather than other classes of information. The two have to be carefully distinguished.

There are certain other interesting facts about the arousal system that have implications for the central topic of this book. One is that the sensory input most effective in raising the level of arousal is touch and the least effective is vision, but all locations of touch do not produce equal results. The touching of the head produces the most marked arousal effects. This finding, again, fits well with common experience. The touching of the lips is much more likely to produce excitement than will the touching of the big toe. The flashing and changing lights of the nightclub do little to arouse us from our nocturnal torpor, but the loud music does.

A final point is that many psychologists have taken the position that effective learning requires an optimum level of arousal. A high degree of excitement is unfavorable for learning because the individual becomes quite disorganized in that state. A low degree of arousal produces a state too near to sleep, where no learning can occur. The argument is that the optimum state of arousal lies between these two extremes. There is evidence to provide some support for this position.

The arousal mechanism has been discussed here for the reason that some of the input from audiovisual materials may serve the purpose of producing arousal rather than of communicating information. This would be particularly true of the auditory material, in that the arousal effects of the visual appear to be minimal. At this point of our knowledge it is perhaps better to state problems than to speculate about answers. An interesting problem to investigate would be whether the use of loud music, designed to produce arousal, might have positive effects on learning through the visual perceptual system. There is also the possibility that such music might not only increase the arousal level but also, at the same time, utilize some of the capacity of the individual for processing information and, hence, reduce learning.

The effect of sensory stimulation on arousal is believed to take place through the neural structure known as the reticular activating system. However, the level of arousal is also dependent on other structures and mechanisms in the central nervous system. For example, the limbic system has to do with the level of excitement or wakefulness.

The Size of a Visual Presentation

A factor of considerable interest that has not been studied in relation to learning is the effect of the size of the visual presentation on learning. A number of observations lead one to conclude that the extent to which the visual presentation fills the retina may be an important variable. Certainly, artists agree that the size of the visual presentation is an important factor in determining the response which a work of art produces. A painting on a canvas 20 feet wide and 9 feet high which the viewer surveys from a distance of 10 feet is likely to have an entirely different effect from that of a small color reproduction of the same painting which appears in a book. The one almost fills the retina, while the other does no more than stimulate a small portion at the center. The effect of a movie shown on a large screen is very different from that of the same movie seen at home on a color-television receiver. The artistic world has no doubt that the filling of the visual world with a display does different things to the viewer than when the same visual image is reduced greatly in size.

A number of different factors would appear to combine to produce this difference. First, the arousal effect of stimulation is probably increased as the number of receptors is increased. Humans like to have a visual field filled with changing elements. A similar effect is shown in the gustatory sense of young children, who like to fill their mouths to the point where all the widely distributed taste receptors become stimulated. In the case of the child, these taste receptors are widely distributed over the entire interior of the mouth; hence, packing the mouth full with flavorsome food produces a massive stimulation of the taste receptors. An adult never has a similar experience with the taste system, since growing up results in the deterioration of these receptors except for those in the tongue region. Massive sensory stimulation, wherever it is possible, is sought after.

Another factor is that the analysis of visual information appears to take place in a somewhat different way for peripheral and central vision, that is, foveal vision. Foveal vision involves a detailed analysis of a small section of the visual field. Peripheral vision, on the other hand, involves a gross analysis. Where the crude analysis of the peripheral information suggests that particularly significant events are happening, then the eye is moved so that the events fall within the foveal region. An optimum condition for utilizing information would appear to be one in which the source of detailed information falls on the fovea and the context information fills other areas of the retina.

Attention, Expectancy of Future Use, and Learning

An important condition for learning is that the would-be learner attend to the input of information. This requirement involves appropriate orienting responses, the clearing of the perceptual system of other information, and the transfer of the information to be retained from the preperceptual field to the perceptual field. These operations will transfer the information to a temporary memory system, as when one looks at the name of a street scrawled on a piece of paper and remembers it long enough to use the information in searching for a particular address. Such information is not likely to become permanently stored, but is rapidly forgotten. The other conditions that have to exist, besides those related to attention, have not been well identified except perhaps for one to be considered now.

Psychologists from William James down to modern times have commonly stated that intent to learn was the crucial factor, in addition to attention, that resulted in learning. This concept of *intent* is quite vague and, because of its intangible nature, psychologists have had difficulty in designing studies in which the effect of intent could be explored. While most of us agree that intent to learn seems to be a significant factor in our own learning, experimental psychologists have not been able to produce evidence to support this position. Recently, Nuttin and Greenwald (1968) have been able to restate this problem in a new form. These workers produced a series of ingenious studies in which they have shown that a crucial factor in learning, at least with verbal materials, is the expectation that the information presented is going to be needed later. In these studies, expectation of future need for the information provided was a far more significant factor in determining whether the information was retained than was reward or punishment.

Although one cannot readily experiment with intent by systematically increasing or decreasing the intent of subjects to learn and thereby study the effect of intent on behavior, one can design experiments in which subjects are exposed to materials and in which some know that they are to use the information supplied later, and others do not expect to. In such experiments one is able to identify clearly such a variable and study the effect it has on learning. A living creature capable of storing in his permanent memory system only that which had a high probability of future utility would have an efficient basis for retaining or discarding information.

Implications for the Design of Audiovisual Materials

The review provided in this chapter makes it clear that there is considerable knowledge available on conditions that facilitate or interfere with attention. Of particular importance is the requirement that the learner not be asked to attend to too much at one time. Equally damaging to the concentration of attention is the situation in which too little information is provided by the instructional device. The designer of audiovisual materials has to attempt to aim somewhere between these two extremes. Attention is most likely to be directed toward those situations for which attention has been rewarded in the past and toward situations that are enjoyable and pleasant. If the teacher wants students to attend to demonstrations as a part of the regular class routine, then these must be made pleasurable and rewarding experiences, as well as moving at a sufficient rate that they provide sufficient information to hold attention. The wakefulness of the subject is to some degree a matter of maintaining an adequate input of information through the perceptual systems.

Although teachers have long viewed the matter of gaining attention as one of the central problems of instruction, the value of attention for producing permanent learning seems to have been overestimated. The kinds of phenomena related to attention that have been discussed can be considered as necessary conditions for effective learning, but they are not sufficient conditions. To rely on attention alone is likely to result in a rather inefficient kind of learning, but attention coupled with activities involving the utilization of information are likely to be much more successful.

Chapter 7

Some Characteristics of Auditory and Visual Instructional Materials

From the Simple to the Complex

The saying has long been embedded in educational literature that the teacher should begin instruction with simple material and slowly move to the complex. This concept of the ordering of education can have many meanings. One is that the teacher can arrange subject matter along a dimension from concepts that are easy to grasp to those that are much more complex and difficult to understand. In the application of this arrangement of subject matter, the teacher of elementary science introduces the concepts of volume and weight, which are readily related to observables, before introducing such concepts as mass, which is highly abstract.

There is also a second meaning of the idea that instruction should proceed from the simple to the complex. In this meaning, more elaborate concepts are built up on the basis of simpler concepts. Thus the concept of division appears to involve the concept of subtraction, at least insofar as it is undertaken by arithmetical means. In recognition of this fact, the teacher of elementary mathematics familiarizes the pupil with addition before introducing the concept of arithmetical division. In this case, it is not just that the concept of division is more difficult to grasp than that of addition, but that the concept of division requires a prior understanding of the concept of addition. To some small degree, some of the concepts in all disciplines can be arranged in a hierarchy, so that the concepts higher up in the hierarchy can be understood only after certain concepts lower down have already been mastered. Not all concepts can be arranged in this way and, in the less developed disciplines, very little organization of this kind is possible.

There is also a third way in which subject matter can be arranged from the simple to the complex. In this method, the same subject matter is first taught through the use of simple analogies and then taught, at a later date, through more direct and sophisticated means. Electricity may first be understood through the use of the analogy which compares the electric current to the flow of water in a pipe. Later the concept of the electron is introduced and, at a still later stage, the concept of energy levels of atomic structure. Most scientific concepts are taught through such an evolution from simple analogy to sophisticated explanation.

Finally, there is still another way in which subject matter can be classified as simple or complex. An example of this fourth meaning is presented by biology, where the subject matter can be taught through a direct study of living matter or through simplified diagrams in which all but the essential features have been eliminated from the presentation. Thus one may teach the functions of the components of cells through the direct examination of living and stained cells in which the relevant matters discussed are difficult to observe, or through simplified diagrams of cells in which all nonessential elements have been eliminated. It is this latter form of simplification with which we are concerned here.

An a priori analysis of the situation leads one to suppose that there should be great advantages to the simplification of visual materials for the purposes of instruction. The information-analysis system described in this book presents the visual perceptual system as one which provides an analysis of visual data by much discarding of the least important aspects of a visual display and the analysis of salient characteristics. In addition, the physiological mechanisms would also appear to involve the simplification of visual information, with the discarding of the least significant features, the redundant features, and the noisy features. This description suggests that learning, and particularly perceptual learning, might be substantially facilitated through the simplification of those visual displays produced for instructional purposes. The idea is that a visual display which emphasizes only the significant features should facilitate learning, in that the learner would not have to devote his energies to making discriminations between the significant and the nonsignificant features in the information input. This hypothesis not only has a high degree of plausibility, but also represents a prejudice commonly found among teachers who frequently use simplified representations of phenomena in their teaching.

Overing and Travers (1966, 1967) conducted two experiments to obtain some data about this matter so vital to the design of audiovisual materials. The essence of the experiments was that the principle of refraction was taught to groups of pupils in the upper elementary-school grades under a number of different conditions. All pupils heard the same description of the phenomenon given through a tape recorder, but the supplementary materials were varied. In the case of some pupils, the supplementary materials involved a fish tank of water and a real beam of light that could be seen entering the tank and bending where it obliquely struck the surface of the water. Other pupils saw the same phenomenon presented through diagrams. Still others learned only from the verbal material alone. The expectation was that the visual presentation involving the verbal materials plus the diagrams would produce a more effective learning situation than the situation involving the fish tank together with considerable paraphernalia necessary for projecting a beam of light obliquely onto the surface of the water. It should be noted that, in order to make the beam of light clearly visible, a small amount of milk was added to the water, and the air was filled with dust from a chalk eraser. There can be no doubt that the demonstration was clear and unambiguous and did not suffer from a lack of visibility of the phenomenon involved.

The extent to which learning occurred as a result of exposure to visual and auditory material was measured through the performance of the subjects on two tasks involving an application of the principle of refraction to a practical situation. The situation was adapted from the original task, used by Charles Judd in his famous experiment on the transfer of training, of aiming a gun at an object immersed beneath the surface of water. The task involved the aiming but not the shooting of a dummy pistol. It eliminated the unreliability produced by differences in level of skill in actual shooting technique, in that the subjects were simply asked to indicate the point on the surface of the water at which they were firing. It was possible for subjects to do so because the surface of the water was covered with a plastic grid on which numbered lines were drawn. Thus the subject might report that he was firing at the line marked 7 or the line marked 6. The subjects never actually fired a shot. In order to control the angle of fire, the dummy pistol was held on a stand at a given height from the ground and the subject was free to rotate the pistol to fire at different points on the surface of the water. Each subject was required to undertake two such tasks. On each task the subject "fired" successive shots and was told after each that he had missed the target area, hit it, or hit a "bull's eye," that is, the center of the target. Each subject had 12 trials in which to hit the bull's eye. If he hit the bull's eye before his twelfth trial, the series was terminated.

The Superiority of Realistic Training Situations

In the first of the two studies under consideration (Overing & Travers, 1966), the results showed that training in the realistic situation, that is, in the situation involving many irrelevant features, tended to produce better learning than did training in a situation in which simplified drawings were used. However, an additional feature had been introduced into one of the treatments that helps to explain the experimental results. In the case of one group that received instruction from the drawings, the pupils were given a brief orientation to the learning situation by a discussion of the problem faced by an explorer who was attempting to shoot a crocodile 3 feet below the surface of the water and 20 feet from the bank where the explorer stood. It was pointed out to these pupils that the explorer would not be able to hit the crocodile by aiming his gun directly but would have to aim at a point above where the crocodile appeared to be located. Children who were given this prior orientation were able to learn from the diagrams about as effectively as those who were exposed to the realistic display.

Several factors appear to account for the results of this study. One is that children exposed to the diagrammatic drawings seem to have difficulty in linking up the knowledge they acquire with a practical situation, and hence have difficulty in making an application of their knowledge to a practical situation. This is not the only factor that accounts for the superiority of the realistic situation. Another factor stems from the fact that in the task of shooting at a target under water, the subject must be able to recognize what are relevant features from what are irrelevant features of the situation in which he has to solve a problem. If he has already been trained in a realistic situation, he has had some practice in making this discrimination, for the realistic situation is filled with irrelevant detail, but training in the situation involving the diagrams provides him with no such experience. In order to test the latter hypothesis, another experiment was conducted (Overing & Travers, 1967).

In this second experiment two different training situations were used. Although both training situations used a tank and a beam of light as a part of the instructional procedure, in the one case no attempt was made to reduce or eliminate irrelevant features of the demonstration. However, in the other training situation every effort was made to eliminate irrelevant features. Black screens were used to hide from view irrelevant aspects of the apparatus. The source of light, the dust-making apparatus, and other features which were unimportant for understanding the phenomenon were out of view and the subject saw little else than a beam of light bending as it entered the water. Thus two training situations were developed, one of which provided a wealth of irrelevant detail and the other eliminated, as far as possible, all irrelevant detail. The tests for learning also involved two levels of irrelevant detail. In the one case the subject had to shoot at a simple cross placed on the bottom of the tank. In the other case, involving irrelevant detail, the subject shot at a target surrounded with irrelevant detail and the grid at which he shot was red and blue, in contrast to the grid in the simplified situation that was only blue. The results showed that those who had been trained in a situation involving many irrelevancies were capable of handling both the testing situation involving embellishment and the one involving little embellishment. However, those who had been trained in the situation involving few irrelevant cues had difficulty in handling the test situation involving many irrelevant cues, though they performed as well as the other groups in the situations that had few irrelevancies.

What these data show is that a person trained in a situation similar to what may be called a realistic situation, that is, a situation involving many irrelevancies, is able to transfer his learning to other situations involving *different* irrelevancies. However, while the person trained in a simplified situation is able to transfer his knowledge to other problems involving a few irrelevancies, he has difficulty in making transfer to situations in which many new irrelevancies are involved. The data provide considerable support for the position that learning undertaken in the setting simulating the real world, with all the natural confusions that real-life situations involve, is a somewhat better preparation for handling the problems of a real world than is learning undertaken in artificial situations that have been grossly simplified for instructional purposes. A qualification to this conclusion is that when the simplified situation is verbally related to a concrete situation, then the disadvantages of the simplified presentation tend to be reduced.

The data in the studies that have been reported raise a number of issues central to the design of audiovisual materials. Textbooks in the audiovisual field have long proclaimed the virtues of realistic materials, in contrast to the symbolic, although the rationale underlying the premise does not appear to have been worked out. The main argument in favor of the use of realistic materials would appear to run along the following lines.

Children learn first, it may be argued, about a real world. They cannot learn to utilize symbols and language until the symbols and the language have some tie with the world of direct experience. Hence, as a general rule, learning has to proceed from initial contacts with the real world to symbolic representations of that real world. Up to a point, this argument is sound, but it is going too far to generalize and to take the position that all learning has to proceed in this order. Consider, for example, the learning situation involved in the teaching of the principle of refraction. Why does it seem desirable to provide a demonstration of refraction in a realistic setting or to relate an abstract presentation to a realistic setting? Children already know what a fish tank looks like, and they are familiar with beams of light, having seen the sun shine through a crack into a room with dust-laden air. They should be able to understand clearly and unequivocally exactly what is meant by a beam of light striking the surface of water and bending as it enters the fluid. Their background of experience is sufficient so that the abstract presentation should present no problems to them at all. But it does present problems.

Two factors have already been mentioned which may account for a part of the superiority of realistic teaching situations. One of these is the fact that the realistic situation permits the learner to exercise skill in discriminating between relevant and irrelevant details. Another is the importance of providing a learning situation that permits a hookup of the world of symbolic events with the world of phenomenal experience. Application of symbolic knowledge would appear to require that such a hookup take place, and it seems that the hookup is not likely to take place unless either the learning situation encourages it or the relationship is already pointed out. There would also appear to be a third factor that might give advantage to the realistic-demonstration type of learning situation, although we do not have evidence at this time to substantiate the importance of this factor. Reference is made here to the fact that a realistic demonstration of a phenomenon permits the learner to obtain multiple views from different directions of what is involved. When multiple views of a situation are obtained by an observer, more information about the situation can be obtained than from a single view of the situation. Sound-motion pictures can accomplish this multiplicity to some extent by providing views of events from different angles, but there is still a difference between the film situation and the realistic situation. In the realistic situation the learner can choose the particular perspectives that he wants to view. As he obtains knowledge of the situation, he can add to his knowledge systematically by searching out particular items of information he needs. There is a fundamental difference between being spoon-fed and feeding oneself.

There is also another important, and related, difference in the two situations. Only recently have psychologists pointed out the importance for efficient learning of permitting animals to manipulate or come into contact with the stimuli they are being trained to discriminate. Lovejoy (1968) points out that the early experimenters who attempted to train animals to discriminate vertical lines from horizontal lines, or black squares from white squares, generally failed to do so. However, later experimenters showed that failure to learn was not due to the inherent stupidity of the animals, but to the ignorance of the trainer. Discriminations can be readily learned by rats and other mammals provided the animal is trained in a situation in which it has direct stimulus contact with the object involved in the discrimination. Such contact is provided by a learning situation in which the rat must push open the door carrying the black square or the white circle. Such a situation brings the animal into close contact with the stimulus which it is learning to discriminate from other stimuli. Probably much the same is true, but to a lesser extent, in the case of young children. Children do learn by exposure to stimuli, but contact with and manipulation of the stimuli improve the learning.

Lovejoy also uses related facts and findings from the history of psychology to support the contention that in such tasks as are typically found in discrimination-learning experiments, the animal is not learning responses but is learning to select stimuli to which to respond. This is an old controversy in psychology, but Lovejoy musters strong support for the position that the animal learns to select stimuli and does not learn responses.

The importance of manipulating the environment in learning situations is also brought out in experiments with both animals and humans, in which the learner either is given an opportunity to learn about the environment by being moved around it or has the opportunity to learn by making his own movements and moving himself around the environment. In such experiments, learning takes place more effectively when the individual moves himself than when he is moved. This is very much like the difference in learning to find one's way around a town, between driving oneself and being driven; the person who is driven generally learns very little. Most audiovisual materials provide learning in a situation in which the learner is a static observer and has no opportunities for making responses.

A final point to note is that realistic demonstrations of phenomena also provide one additional advantage over film or videotape demonstrations. This is the advantage that stems from the fact that a realistic demonstration permits the viewer to ask what would happen if a certain change were made in the demonstration. The changes can then be made and the effect on the phenomenon observed. In other words, such demonstrations permit active experimentation. The film substitute, in which the narrator asks what would be the effect of a particular change and then demonstrates the effect of such a change, can hardly be expected to encourage the viewer to think for himself and to conjure up significant questions. The difference in the learning value of situations in which the learner exercises control and in which the teacher exercises control has long been deemphasized by writers in the audiovisual field, and yet it is one of fundamental importance. An audiovisual presentation of information probably cannot be as effective as a realistic demonstration. Audiovisual materials are not just substitutes for the realistic materials; they are different from the realistic materials. They have their place in learning, but we still have only the most limited conception of the conditions under which they can be most effectively used.

Symbolic Materials and the Age of the Learner

The point must also be raised here that a crucial factor in determining the extent to which instructional situations can be designed entirely in symbolic terms is probably the age of the pupil. Every major psychologist who has written about the developmental pattern has taken the position that as children grow older they become more and more capable of learning from strictly symbolic material. The earlier writers tended to take a more optimistic view about the capability of young children learning effectively from symbolic materials, but more recent writers have taken a pessimistic position. The data presented indicate a surprising inability of 12- and 13-year-olds in handling a situation in abstract terms, a finding that fits the general position taken here that educators have overestimated the ability of pupils in this respect.

Nevertheless, some data demonstrate that young children have a surprising ability to use abstract and simplified materials under some circumstances. A recent study by Travers (1969) that involved teaching a concept to nursery-school children provided one such surprise. In this study the young children were taught the concept of a half. To achieve this purpose, each child was taken to a corner of a classroom to play a game. In the first part of the game the child was given an explanation of the concept of a half through the use of materials in which some pictures showed objects cut in half, and others cut into other fractions. Half of the children were taught using representations of real objects such as apples, bananas, and so forth. The other children were taught the same concept, but with abstract materials consisting of colored squares, triangles, and ovals. All children were then tested for their knowledge of the concept with a 20-item test, of which 10 items consisted of pictures of real objects and 10 of abstract shapes. In the test materials some of the objects were cut in half, and some were cut into other fractions. The performances of the children on the test were closely comparable for those trained with the realistic materials and those trained with abstract materials. The effectiveness of the abstract materials in the case of children who were so young was quite a surprising finding. The effectiveness of these materials can, perhaps, be attributed to the fact that children raised in a civilized environment are surrounded with geometric shapes that they learn to identify at an early age. The child who lives in a carpentered environment is probably able to abstract from it, at quite an early age, concepts of form that he can utilize in the tasks required in this study.

The Still Picture as a
Simplified Representation of Action

The typical illustration in a textbook, although a still picture, represents a moving, ongoing scene. A picture of Galileo showing his telescope to an incredulous colleague has meaning only if one understands what Galileo himself has already seen with the instrument and what his colleague will see when he looks through it. A picture of a racing car on the Salt Lake Flats is not the picture of a stationary vehicle, although it is a static picture. It is a picture of a car traveling at great speed toward a finish line outside of the picture. A person who saw it as as a stationary car with fuzzy wheels and a cloud of dust behind it would have missed the entire point of the illustration. Nearly all illustrations in textbooks are attempts to provide the reader with the experience of viewing a dynamic, moving scene, but through the medium of a stationary picture that actually has no motion to it whatsoever. Occasionally a textbook picture presents a static scene, as when a biology book shows a picture of a fossil, but such static pictures are rare and of quite limited utility.

Most illustrations are, then, simplifications of an ongoing scene. They can have significance to a viewer insofar as he can recognize that there were events that led up to the flash of experience represented by the picture and that the illustration leads into a future which includes other events that have to be imagined. Even common scenes generally have to be interpreted by providing them with both a past and a future. A painting of a seashore, with a wave about to break, would be an uninterpretable picture for a person who had never been near a large body of water. But if the painting is well done, and if the viewer is thoroughly familiar with waves breaking on the shore, then he will view the painted seascape as a part of an ongoing scene with the waves rolling toward the shoreline and breaking on the beach. The still picture in the typical textbook initiates a complex experience in the child who sees it, not as a still picture, but more as a motion picture. This may well be the reason why instruction involving filmstrips or other still pictures generally appears to be about as effective as instruction from motion pictures. Still pictures are, in a sense, simplified motion pictures. It is just that they require work on the part of the learner to convert them from static demonstrations to dynamic demonstrations. The properties of still pictures that give them the characteristics of a changing moving scene are referred to here as the *dynamic* properties of pictures.

The fact that most illustrations require such a complex perceptual interpretation to be meaningful suggests that considerable perceptual skill has to be acquired before dynamic interpretations can be introduced. In the Travers (1969) study of picture interpretation in young children, the 4-year-old group was able to identify some specific element in each of the pictures shown, but dynamic interpretations generally require that many elements be identified and interrelated. In order to see a man running in a picture, it is not enough to identify his red coat, the kind of characteristic that a 4-year-old might identify and recall. Cues indicating running include the forward slope of the body, the fact that one foot or both feet are off the ground, and the representation in the picture of a posture that cannot be maintained more than momentarily. The picking up of such cues is a sophisticated intellectual task that is probably beyond the powers of a 4-year-old. At this time little is known about the age at which such cues can be picked up or the extent to which training can lower this age. One suspects that the development of these abilities may be closely tied to the development of the child's information capacity which, in turn, may be highly dependent upon the age of the child. This is a matter that needs to be studied by those interested in the use of pictures with young children.

An interesting related item of information has been reported to me by Marie Hughes, who has made some observations on the use of pictures with young children. Dr. Hughes has observed that the first step that children have to take in learning to use pictures is that of developing an understanding that pictures can represent real objects and that one can learn from pictures much as one learns from real objects. Many children from impoverished homes who first come to school have not yet grasped this fundamental fact and have to learn it.

In the Travers study under consideration, there were a number of other findings of interest in the present connection. One of these was that colored pictures were more readily seen as representing dynamic ongoing events than were black-and-white pictures. Color seems to give a lively quality to pictures, perhaps because such pictures are nearer to being lifelike than any other pictures. Color cues make it possible to relate the pictures to real-life situations and to see them as a part of an ongoing reality.

A substantial research literature brings out a related point. Children in the lower elementary grades *prefer* pictures that are faithful representations of objects and colors encountered in the real world to pictures that are either stylized or sketchy or unrealistic in coloring. This preference for realistic pictures does not mean that the children necessarily learn more from such illustrations, though they probably do. What this finding almost certainly means is that illustrations that are faithful reproductions of the real world are more readily perceived in meaningful terms than are illustrations that are unfamiliar in style, form, or color. Young children have difficulty enough in interpreting pictures that involve lifelike representations, but their task is made immensely more difficult when they have to interpret pictures that are the fanciful representations of the artists. All too often, textbooks for the lower elementary grades are replete with artists' sketches that are far from being realistic representations of the subject illustrated. Such illustrations probably do much to sell the books to textbook committees but contribute little to the education of the child.

Chapter 8

The Human Memory Systems

Mention has already been made of the fact that two temporary memory systems exist. The first of these has been referred to as the *memory trace*. It is a very short-term system, holding information for only a few seconds. In addition, there is a short-term memory system that is commonly believed to hold information for perhaps as long as 30 minutes. Some doubt exists whether the short-term memory system is continuous with and a part of the *permanent memory system*. Evidence on this point is conflicting, and we have made the arbitrary decision here to treat the short-term memory system separately from the permanent memory system.

Memory, Storage, and Retrieval

The long-term memory system almost certainly involves the storage of information at the synapses, the positions where the extensions of the one nerve cell come into promixity with extensions from other nerve cells. These synapses function as on-off switches in that they either permit a nerve impulse to pass across the gap or they block the impulse. The information that is received is finally stored in on-off patterns of these biological switches. We do not know how the information that comes in through the perceptual systems is coded into a series of on-off states of the synapses and is hence permanently stored, but this conversion of the information almost certainly has to take place.

This brings us to a second important point about the long-term storage system, namely, that the person has very little awareness of how information is stored. The problems of what is stored and how it is stored have to be explored by very indirect means. One does not know, for example, whether verbal information is stored in a form similar to perceived speech or in a form similar to words as they appear on a printed page. One has almost no awareness of the extent to which one stores information in terms of words or in terms of other means. Information can be retrieved from the storage system as when one remembers the name of an acquaintance or repeats the words of a familiar poem, but one is quite unaware of how the information has been stored. One is aware of retrieval, but not of storage.

A third general point to note about the memory system is that storage does not involve the kind of system that engineers design. The efficiently designed engineering system of information storage is exemplified by the design of the computer memory. In such a system, one piece of information is stored in one particular place that has a specific address much as an apartment in a building has a specific address. In a computer, a piece of information is stored in one place and in only one place. The brain does not store information in terms of this kind of plan. Evidence suggests that the brain stores the same piece of information in multiple localities. Such a system of storage is suggested by the fact that injury to a particular part of the adult brain does not produce a loss of particular items of information. Indeed, very large areas of the adult brain may be destroyed without the individual having any difficulty in remembering items he has learned. This kind of evidence strongly suggests multiple storage and a system which makes it impossible to destroy a particular piece of information by destroying a particular locality.

The advantages of a multiple system of storage are substantial. From the biological point of view, it means that local damage does not result in the loss of particular items of learned information which may, perhaps, be vital for survival. Of rather great significance is the fact that a multiple storage system makes it easier to relate a particular item of information to large numbers of other items. From a psychological viewpoint, one does appear to have a system in which particular items of information tend to be associated with a large number of other items. Words are readily associated with numerous other words, and one idea stimulates the recall of a wide range of other ideas. Indeed, knowledge appears to represent an extraordinary network of interrelated items rather than a set of isolated and separately stored items.

Several lines of evidence suggest that there is a retrieval system which functions quite independently of the memory system. There is an accumulating body of evidence that the memory system shows relatively little deterioration as the adult ages, but that the retrieval system deteriorates and causes the familiar lapses of memory of the elderly. A retrieval system would appear to be necessary in order that the entire system of recorded memories does not have to be scanned in sequence for the recovery of any particular item. One presumes that the retrieval system makes decisions concerning where to look in the files of experience. A particularly puzzling phenomenon is reflected in the fact that the retrieval system appears to know whether or not it is worthwhile looking for a particular piece of information. In other words, we search in our memory system for a piece of information which we are sure that we have even though it cannot be readily recalled. We know that the information is there although we cannot recover it immediately. This phenomenon suggests that the retrieval system has some kind of inventory of what is stored in permanent memory. However, an alternative, but closely related explanation is possible. Consider, for example, the case in which one encounters a person on the street. One knows that one knows his name, but cannot recall it at the time. What may be happening in one's retrieval system is this. One is familiar with the person one encounters, and hence one makes the inference that one must also know his name. In order to make this inference, one has to have knowledge of some general rule such as "If one knows a person, one also knows his name." On the basis of such a rule, one can decide whether or not one is likely to have stored the name of a person one encounters. The retrieval system may decide to search or not to search the permanent memory system on the basis of this kind of rule.

Some Characteristics of the Long-Term Memory System

Before considering various theoretical positions of what is stored, some comments must be made concerning a few important characteristics of the retention system.

First, it seems clear that man has only a limited ability to store uncoded incoming information. For example, portrait painters apparently have only the most restricted ability to store visual information about the subject they are painting. Indeed, such artists insist that the subject sit for them on a very large number of different occasions. If the artist were capable of remembering the details of the visual representation, a long series of sittings would be quite unnecessary for he could do most of his work from memory. While artists are those whom one would expect to have excellent memories for visual information, they apparently do not have this capacity. The direct retention of visual information which has not been coded can occur to only a limited degree. Comparable situations calling for the retention of uncoded auditory information are difficult to find. A musician who listens to a new melody and who later is able to play it on the piano may not be dealing with uncoded information. What he does in retaining this information is not well understood, but he could well store the information in terms of the written musical notation code customarily used by musicians. A few pieces of auditory information, after much practice, can be reproduced with great precision, as when a naturalist imitates the call of a wild animal. The ability to do this is extremely rare, but those who do it perform only very short and repetitive types of calls.

The examples we have just considered are to be contrasted with man's extraordinary capacity to learn and retain verbal information. The retention is often not only of large quantities of information, but in great detail. A Shakespearean actor may know the part of Hamlet perfectly to the last detail. In addition, he may know most of the other Shakespearean parts as well. The capacity of the verbal memory appears to be large and to provide a precise record. As another example of the verbal memory, consider man's capacity to learn speech. A person may have a vocabulary of 50,000 words or more in his native tongue, and also know almost as many words in several other tongues. The memory system has a considerable capacity for this kind of information even though it is a limited-capacity system.

Some information is available concerning the form of information held in the verbal memory system. The trend of a whole series of studies suggests that printed visual material tends to be recoded into auditory information. A particularly striking demonstration of this phenomenon can be found in a study by Wickelgren (1965b), in which lists of printed letters were to be remembered. When subjects made errors of memory, the errors involved the reprodution of letters similar in sound to those that should have been reproduced, rather than letters that were similar in appearance. In two other studies, Wickelgren (1965a, 1966) showed the recall of printed letters, presented visually, was interfered with by the presentation of other letters that had to be copied immediately before or after the letters that had to be remembered. The confusion produced in the memory task by the copying task depended upon the extent to which the names for the letters to be copied resembled *in sound* the names for the letters to be memorized. Another interesting and related item of information was turned up by Corcoran (1967), who showed that when subjects were asked to scan a page of print and to cross out every letter *e*, they tended to miss the silent *e* in *es*. It is as if the visual information is converted to an auditory trace before it is scanned, so that when the auditory trace lacked an *e* sound then the *e* was missed.

This kind of evidence suggests that, in the case of at least some material, the visual information received is recoded into an auditory form of information and is retained in this form, at least in short-term memory. If the information were to be retained in long-term memory, it hardly seems likely that it would be recoded again into a form that in some direct way represented visual information. This leads us to the interesting speculation that much of the long-term memory system may involve the storage of auditory verbal information.

There is also some evidence suggesting that the retention of non-verbal visual information is facilitated through providing some kind of label for the visual display (see Travers & Chan, 1966). We do not know whether a person customarily undertakes such verbal recoding in order to facilitate retention. For example, when a person visits a cathedral, is he helped in retaining information about the structure by saying to himself that the style is "perpendicular Gothic"? One suspects that this form of recoding is enormously important and accounts for the fact that the expert on architecture is able to retain much after a single viewing of a structure, while the unsophisticated viewer can retain only the roughest features of what he has seen. The unsophisticated viewer is able to retain only crude information, probably because his vocabulary is crude. On the other hand, the architect has a complex and well-developed vocabulary in terms of which he can code and remember a great complexity of detail. Without such recoding, he would be no better off than the portrait artist who is unable to retain essential information about the model he is attempting to present on canvas.

The evidence we have been discussing suggests that the human permanent memory system is mainly a verbal memory system. Incoming information, if it is to be effectively stored, is recoded as verbal information before it is placed in the storage system. Certainly, one would expect that any encouragement given to the learner to verbalize and talk about the experiences he wishes to remember would facilitate the retention of information related to those experiences.

Primitive Forms of Long-Term Memory

One is readily tempted to make the generalization that all human memory is in the form of verbal material related to the auditory mode, but such a conclusion is unreasonable. Subhuman primates, with almost no verbal capacity at all, are able to retain considerable quantities of information which obviously cannot be coded into a verbal form for permanent storage; storage has to be related to something more closely akin to the visual image or auditory image. One can reasonably assume that man also has this kind of crude primitive memory, though the information stored in that system is vastly overwhelmed and overshadowed by the large amount of information in the verbal storage system. Indeed, one suspects that in those persons interviewed by Francis Galton who claimed that they did not have any visual imagery, the primitive memory mechanism may be functioning at a minimal level. Various terms have been used to describe the representations in this primitive form of memory. In the case of visual memory, the term *icon,* a Greek word denoting some form of pictorial representation, has had a long history. The term *iconic memory* was first used by the philosopher C. S. Peirce in the nineteenth century. No corresponding term has become widely accepted for the case of crude auditory memories. The term *echo* has been used to refer to a crude auditory nonverbal memory trace. The term *echoic memory* has been applied to a primitive memory system involving the storage of these auditory records.

The theory that images are stored in a form that makes it possible for the viewer to revive them and re-experience them has been attractive to thinkers through several hundred years of history, but it is far too simple to account for events even in a relatively primitive memory system. Although it is clear that general ideas can be stored in terms of words, the problem of whether the crude memory system is able to store information representing a general class of objects has been a much more difficult matter to investigate.

The issue is an old one in the fields both of philosophy and psychology. The school of philosophers known as the British Empiricists debated at length whether an idea in a form other than a word could represent a general idea. The issue was whether one can have an internal representation of, say, a tree, that is not just a representation of a particular tree. The issue is much like the contemporary debate about whether one's memory records numerous specific experiences or consolidations of those experiences.

The concept of a schema developed by Head (1920) was later picked up by Bartlett (1932), who popularized it in psychological literature. While it still remained a fuzzy concept, Bartlett also tied it in closely with a response component. Schemata, for him, modified both the interpretation of sensory data and responses. His position is confused by his contention that schemata are organizations of both "past reactions" and "past experiences" (Bartlett, 1932, p. 201). Whether the organizations of "past reactions" are organizations of the kinesthetic and other experiences that accompany behavior or are something more akin to habit hierarchies is not clear.

The early workers in the area of memory, such as Bartlett, failed to give adequate recognition to the extent to which experience is recoded into words before it is stored. For this reason, they gave undue emphasis to the role that imagery, or related schemata, plays in the retention of experience. Many of their experiments involved the use of diagrams and other related visual materials that were probably retained as images. However, the more recent work on imagery strongly suggests that it is a very inferior memory system. For example, some quite recent work by Hebb (1968) on imagery generally conforms to the belief that information stored in images is generally quite imprecise. Even those adults who report relatively good imagery are not generally able to read off from it any details that they had not previously noted. The evidence suggests that the image is a crude and primitive memory form of very limited value to persons living in a complex society that requires the individual to store considerable amounts of information in considerable detail. Perhaps this is why the most educated members of such societies report the least amount of imagery.

Speculation in this area is easily led astray by personal experience. The fact that one can report images leads one to assume that the storage is in a form in the nervous system closely related to the production of images. Those who speculate in this area have commonly assumed that an image is produced through the activity of a particular neural circuit and that the image is stored in the synapses in this particular neural circuit. This is a conception that Hebb has long proposed (1949), but the evidence to support such a position is lacking and alternatives to such a conception exist.

An alternative hypothesis is that crude memories are not stored in the form of images at all, but that the experience of an image occurs because the image has been synthesized from other more rudimentary materials. This is not entirely a clear concept, but it can be clarified through an analogy. A computer can produce, almost instantaneously, any logarithm of any number to any base. If one wants to know the logarithm of 5 to the base 2 to 24 decimal places, the computer will print this logarithm out in short order, despite the fact that it does not store logarithms. What the computer does, instead of storing logarithms, is to store a rule for calculating logarithms, and with this rule it can produce any logarithm at any time. Logarithms are synthesized, and not stored. Perhaps the same thing occurs when one experiences an image. The image may be synthesized rather than stored, but just how this synthesis takes place one cannot readily imagine at the present time; nevertheless, it is not outside the realm of possibility.

A final point must be made in relation to primitive memory systems. There is, in a sense, an even more primitive kind of memory system than that we have been considering. Memory at a very primitive level involves no more than the retention of particular responses to be made to particular objects. Very simple approach and avoidance responses would be of this order, as illustrated by the child who puts out his hand to grasp a cookie or who withdraws from a particular object that has caused pain. Very simple approach and avoidance responses require only the establishment of direct connections between the inputs and the outputs. Although most responses in the human involve complex internal processes that intervene between the input and the response, there are some, particularly in children, that do not involve such complexities and call for only a very simple retention system.

One must assume that the acquisition of many common motor skills represents retention at this kind of level. The rider of a bicycle can make the adjustments necessary to keep himself right side up to the world, and these adjustments he makes with great rapidity. He does not have time to make them slowly, with much thought taking place. Indeed, success in riding a bicycle requires that the appropriate responses occur with only a very minimum delay. In order for this to happen, there must be a very direct connection between situations to be handled by particular responses and the response mechanisms that produce the responses. This does not mean that the neural structures involved are not very complex; for they are, but they do exclude the operation of thought processes which enter into other aspects of human behavior that involve stored verbal information.

 The Transfer to Permament Memory

Most of the information that enters the short-term memory system never becomes permanently stored. This fact is to man's advantage for, in this way, the permanent memory system is protected from becoming cluttered with a mass of detail that has only transitory value. We watch the unfolding scene that life brings us in our daily rounds, but most of it represents information that has no lasting value. The short-term memory retains the information of the moment just long enough for us to be able to use it. In the chitchat that takes place over a cup of coffee, we remember what was said a few minutes back and retain enough of it to maintain the thread of the conversation, but we are likely to forget about the entire conversation before the day is out. If information is to be placed in the permanent memory system, considerable effort is likely to be expended. This expenditure of effort is generally directed along two main lines.

First, information placed many times in temporary storage is likely to be remembered permanently. This activity is what the student performs when he tries to master the vocabulary of a foreign language. He reads through the list of foreign words and their English equivalents many times a day. The permanent memory system would be efficiently stored with useful information if it had transferred to it any information that entered the short-term memory system on several occasions. This would be the information most commonly needed.

Second, information that is known to be needed at some future time is also likely to be transferred from short-term memory to long-term memory. As was pointed out earlier, this is an important component of what writers used to refer to as intent to learn. Attempts to provide practice with using the material to be learned will probably prove effective if they combine practice together with a forceful demonstration that what is to be mastered has future value. Passive exposures to single experiences do little to transfer the information to which the individual is exposed to the permanent memory system. Yet it is passive experience of this kind that typical audio-visual materials are designed to provide.

The reader may wonder at this point why reinforcement has not been mentioned as a crucial factor in the transfer of information from the short-term memory system to the long-term system. The reason for this exclusion is that contemporary research literature on human memory makes virtually no mention of reinforcement. Adams's (1967) excellent review of research on human memory does not even list reinforcement as a topic in the index to the book, but makes vague reference to it in the text. Writers in the area generally assume that reinforcements determine choices in the matter of what is learned but are quite incidental to the learning process. A person may master a skill or trade because he will make his living from that skill or trade; the reinforcements are in the form of money; the reinforcements are not what produces learning. The transfer of the information to the long-term memory system appears to have only the most indirect relationship to reinforcement. The author recognizes that there are many psychologists with backgrounds in animal psychology who would object to the position taken here and who would give reinforcement a central role in learning, but that is not the position taken by psychologists working either in the field of human memory or verbal learning.

The chief virtue of programed materials of the type that Skinner and his associates have advocated using is that such material requires the learner to use actively the information provided. With each small piece of information provided in the program, there comes also a problem that has to be solved. This system provides a fairly efficient means of transferring information to permanent memory, though it has not resulted in any overwhelming improvement in the efficiency with which pupils learn. Indeed, although this approach to the presentation of materials was hailed, when it was first proposed, as one offering great promise of improving the efficiency of learning, the promise has not been fulfilled. Why such a method demanding great activity on the part of the learner has not brought with it substantial increases in the efficiency of learning is an important question to answer. One possible reason is that the transfer of information to permanent memory is quite a slow process, and attempts to speed the transfer may have little success. There is certainly evidence that the transfer of information to permanent memory takes a substantial time, probably of the order of 20 minutes. This fact can be shown by laboratory studies demonstrating that information to be learned for later recall is peculiarly subject to disruption during the first 20 minutes after attempts are made to learn it. Another source of evidence is that persons who suffer severe concussion typically are unable to remember events that occurred during the 20 minutes preceding the concussion. Such facts are interpreted as indicating that memories of events during the preceding 20 minutes were in the stage of being consolidated in permanent storage when the concussion occurred and were, at that stage, particularly prone to disruption. If memories are disrupted during the consolidation process, then they never become included in the store of permanently retained material.

Most audiovisual materials fail to use any particular strategy to promote the transfer of information to permanent memory. Indeed, most sound-motion pictures or filmstrips with accompanying commentaries are designed on the assumption that an experience with the materials will produce learning. Insofar as these learning experiences provide multiple exposures to the same information, they may result in some transfer of information to permanent memory. However, most of these materials provide what is essentially a single exposure unless run through several times. Some of these materials have been designed so that the information provided has to be utilized by the learner, but most of the difficulties involved in designing such materials have not been worked out.

Cognitive Structures

The permanent memory system differs from a computer memory in one important respect that has already been mentioned, namely, that it does not depend upon a simple address system in which one piece of information is stored at one particular address and at no other. There is also a second important and related feature distinguishing the computer memory from the human memory which has also been mentioned, namely, that what is retained commonly represents a consolidation of inputs rather than a collection of the inputs themselves. A third distinguishing feature is that the information in human memory has organization of a kind simply not found in the information in computer memories. Knowledge is organized, and internal organizations of knowledge are referred to as *cognitive structures,* a term introduced originally by Edward Tolman.

Some of the more obvious aspects of memory reflect commonly recognized organizations of the information stored. One aspect is that information seems to be catalogued in some *temporal sequence.* A football commentator giving a brief summary of the game that has been played has no difficulty in remembering that one particular play came before another. The sequence of plays is readily recalled. Although one may have difficulty, when looking back several years, in recalling which one of two events came first, recent memories appear to be tagged in such a way that their chronology can be readily identified. How they are tagged is not understood at all.

Another common cognitive structure is related to the *arrangement of objects in space*. One knows, for example, how the objects are arranged in the house in which one lives. A knowledge of this arrangement permits one to know where to look for particular objects. Without such a cognitive structure, one would have to scan the entire house in order to find a particular object. Also, when one views a particular section of the house, one realizes that the particular arrangement of the objects is part of a total arrangement of objects of which one has knowledge. As Gibson (1950) has pointed out, one assumes that the part of the world that one sees is continuous with a wider visual world, most of which one cannot see. The memory system has to have some record of the total visual world arranged in three-dimensional space.

Many cognitive structures are developed as a result of exposure to formal schooling. Every school child acquires some knowledge of American history, but if instruction is well organized, he acquires much more than a medley of facts. The knowledge of American history that he acquires is likely to be organized into several different structures. It is organized into a time structure, in that he knows that certain events preceded certain other events. The learning of some key dates may help to give increased precision to the time structure of history, but this matter of learning dates has long been debated. The student's knowledge of history would not be appropriately structured if the only organization involved were a time organization. History can also be organized in terms of the development of civilizations and the emergence of ideas. The study of the history of the United States would be a barren area for a student who did not learn to see it as the history of the development of a modern form of democracy. The ideas on which our present society is based and the emergence of these ideas represent another form of cognitive structure that may be produced by the study of history.

Most information stored in permanent memory is stored within a number of different cognitive structures. For example, a person who knows Archimedes' principle may know the story of the historical circumstances under which it was developed and, hence, know it as an item in the history of science. He may also know it as a contemporary item of scientific information and know its value in establishing the density of objects. Thus his knowledge of Archimedes' principle falls into at least two different cognitive structures. One of the tasks of the efficient teacher is to help the student fit the knowledge he acquires into a number of different cognitive structures, so that the knowledge can be used in a number of different contexts.

External and Internal Storage of Information

All civilizations have had to acquire means of storing information external to the individual, and these means have been intimately associated with the development of graphic forms of communication. Certainly at quite an early stage in the development of civilization, man evolved means of keeping public records pertaining to such matters as the ownership of land, and these must very rapidly have shown themselves to be of much greater practical utility than the records stored in people's heads. Such objective records provided opportunities for verification and agreement. The development of means of recording publicly certain classes of information began to free man from the immense burden of consigning to his permanent memory whatever information he needed for either private or public use.

Although the technology which reached a peak, though perhaps only a temporary peak, in the development of the printing press, should have emancipated man from the slavery of having to memorize very large quantities of information during his period of schooling, such an emancipation did not take place. Indeed, many of our practices in relation to the memorization of material spring from the days before the printing press. Consider, for example, the typical undergraduate lecture, an institution that dates back to the days before the printing press, when the teacher had parchment and papyrus manuscripts to which the students did not have easy access. In those days, since the professor had generally learned by heart the content of the manuscripts, his class presentation involved repeating the content of the documents so that the material became available to the students. Unfortunately, this practice became institutionalized in Western culture and even today, long after books have become generally available, the academic professor continues to mold his behavior after a pattern that ceased to be appropriate when the printing press was invented. The appropriateness of the lecture form is for information that is not readily available or that represents the work of the particular professor involved, but such cases are rare. Unfortunately, much of the work that has been undertaken in the development of the new media has involved adapting these obsolete practices to the new technology. Thus, although the university lecturer could reach only a small audience with his obsolete technique, television permits him to pursue the same outmoded procedure with audiences of immense size.

Modern methods of storing information in a form that is publicly available reduce the need for the internal storage of information, but educational strategies have not yet taken advantage of this fact. Indeed, the trend in modern educational technology has been to devise methods which the engineers hope will result in the memorization of greater amounts of information in less time than was possible by previous methods. The new technology ignores very largely the fact that the need to store information in human memory is far less today than it ever was in the past.

Knowledge stored outside of man's brain can be used by him provided that two conditions exist. First, there must be some system whereby he can retrieve the information without scanning the entire mass of information in storage. A book without an index can be used for obtaining information only by scanning the entire contents. The table of contents may be a help, representing as it does a very primitive retrieval system. The addition of an index would represent a much more sophisticated form of retrieval system. Although the index of a book is not thus designated, it is one of the basic retrieval systems provided at the present time.

Common experience with book indexes shows quite clearly the difficulties involved in the design of retrieval systems and in the planning of education so that the individual stores as little knowledge as possible within himself and as much knowledge in sources outside of himself. One common experience with an index occurs when one wants to look up a topic in a book in which one knows for sure that there is information. An attempt to locate in the index what one assumes to be the appropriate reference term confronts one with a blank. The term is not there, and neither are any related terms. So what one ends up doing is skimming through the entire book until the needed material has been located. The problem described here is one in which the vocabulary used in the retrieval system in the book does not correspond to the vocabulary that the user of the retrieval system has at his disposal. In order for a retrieval system to function effectively, it must utilize the same vocabulary as that of the user.

At the present time, most retrieval systems are produced by highly arbitrary methods that often fail to use suitable vocabularies. The index of a book is generally compiled by the author, who wades through the proofs pulling out any words that seem to denote important topics. The words are then listed alphabetically at the end of the book, together with the page numbers on which the words are found. The selection of the key terms is highly dependent upon the author's knowledge of what terms are widely used in his area, but he is undoubtedly influenced greatly by his own particular word preferences. Retrieval systems based on individualized judgments are hardly likely to be successful.

There are alternative methods of preparing an index, and although these would be much more costly than the present methods, they might make books far more useful as storage and retrieval systems. One alternative method would be to check the words against a word list and to select those words that represent relatively uncommon usage. The index would simply list these words and indicate the pages on which material related to each could be found. Such a procedure would provide a rather lengthy index, and the compilation would probably have to be undertaken by machine methods, but considerable advantages would probably accrue.

The index of a book represents one of the most primitive of all retrieval systems, despite the fact that it is perhaps the most widely used. A more sophisticated retrieval system, though designed only for gross retrieval purposes, is the card catalogue to a library. Through the perusal of a card catalogue, one can identify cards providing information on specialized topics. Such systems fall far short of those that librarians envision for the future. The present aim of those planning the libraries of the future is to develop a system that will permit the user to locate documents containing quite specific pieces of information. The present card catalogue in any college library will help one to locate books on a broad topic, such as anxiety, but is of little help when it comes to narrowing down the search, say, to studies of the effect of anxiety on the achievement of children of elementary-school age. The search and retrieval system of the future will provide a very quick means of locating documents that provide information related to quite specific problems. Such systems are in the stage of development and are mentioned here because of their relevance to education, in that they give man vastly improved access to the information stored externally to himself and hence reduce the amount of information that he has to store internally.

Advanced retrieval systems have been described by Vickery (1965). An essential feature of all such systems is that they involve the development of a special vocabulary of what are called *descriptors*. Such a descriptor language is necessary in order to overcome the difficulties we have already discussed in the use of an index to a book. When the retrieval system is asked a question, the question has to be translated into the appropriate descriptor language. If one asks a question, for example, about what is known about the effect of anxiety on the achievement of children in the elementary grades, the key terms in the question (anxiety, achievement, and elementary grades) have to be translated into the descriptor language. The latter are commonly three- or four-letter terms such as HUKR and STER. These words are then fed to a computer which searches summaries of documents also written in a similar language.

Eidetic Imagery

The idea is widely held that some individuals have what are termed *photographic memories*. Psychologists have also been long intrigued with this idea and have taken some steps to determine whether a rare form of memory of this kind does actually exist. The nearest phenomenon to a photographic memory that has been identified up to this time is that known as *eidetic imagery,* found only in children. Such children, described first in German literature, are referred to as *eidetikers*. The experimental situations through which those children are identified have never been as well developed as they should have been, and thus the evidence concerning the memory feats that they can or cannot perform has not been clearly demonstrated. The frequency of eidetikers in populations of children vary according to the criterion used for identifying them, and perhaps also according to the locality, but it appears to be somewhere between 5 and 10 per cent.

In a common experimental situation on eidetic imagery, children are shown a picture for a brief time and then, after the picture has been removed, they are asked to report on what they saw in the picture. The eidetikers report far more detail than do typical children and also report that they can see a vivid representation of the picture in front of them in their imagination. What seems to happen is that the stimulus trace persists in the eidetiker and, since it does not rapidly fade, can be used for reading off considerable quantities of information. The reader will remember the experiment of Sperling (1960), described earlier, which showed that, in adults, information could be read from the trace for about 2 seconds but not much longer. In the eidetiker, the trace is present for a much longer time, and information can be read from it for periods far beyond the usual 2 seconds. What this fact suggests is that the eidetiker has difficulty in erasing the trace, and the phenomenon may be a result of the retarded development of the erasure mechanism.

So far no research evidence exists to suggest that the eidetiker has any special advantages in learning in school. Indeed, one may well hypothesize that eidetic imagery produces problems in that different traces might become confused one with another. There is a little evidence that such a fusion of traces does occur.

The Permanence of Storage in Long-Term Memory

An interesting question concerns the extent to which information held in the long-term memory system is stored permanently. This has turned out to be a very hard question to answer because it is difficult to distinguish between the loss of information from the memory system and the inability to retrieve information from it. Everyone has had the experience of being unable to retrieve information that he knows is there. Indeed, he can often later demonstrate that the information was there when it suddenly comes to mind. Failure in the retrieval system is particularly common in old people, but all of us experience failures of retrieval, or lapses of memory as they are called—from the stage-struck child who forgets his poem to the adult who blocks on a name in making an introduction. If man's retrieval system were perfect, then there would be little difficulty in finding out whether the long-term memory system provided permanent storage.

Some psychologists have taken the position that what is learned is permanently learned, but difficulties may occur in the retrieval. These psychologists have generally based their case on two kinds of evidence. One of these, particularly favored by clinical psychologists, is that hypnosis can often be used to produce recall of events which the person claims to have completely forgotten. Under hypnosis, the retrieval system seems to work with extraordinary efficiency, but this does not mean that anything previously learned can be retrieved by hypnosis. The users of hypnosis tend to report the positive instances in which the supposedly forgotten information was recovered under hypnosis. There are certainly many cases in which the hypnotist has been unable to help a client recover important information. Hypnosis may give a temporary tune-up to the retrieval system, but this does not mean that the long-term memory system is a permanent memory system.

A second approach that has led some to believe that whatever is learned is learned permanently comes from studies in which the exposed brains of surgical patients have been stimulated and the patient has been asked to tell what memories the stimulation produced. This can be done without the patient suffering pain or real discomfort, for a portion of the skull is removed under anesthesia and the surface of the brain lacks any pain sensitivity. Electrical stimulation of some of the surfaces produces the revival of the most vivid memories of past events. This kind of recall is generally in terms of images that provide a great wealth of detail. Indeed, the persons involved often claim that by this means they are able to recall details that they had not observed at the time of the original incident. Just how such evidence should be evaluated is not clear at this time. It seems very unlikely that the brain is able to record a very large amount of detail in a form related to images, for most research on images shows them to be very vague structures. There is a possibility that the image having detail may be stored, but that the retrieval system is ordinarily not able to reach it. A much more likely possibility is that the detailed images, experienced by those whose brains are stimulated electrically, may well be reconstructions of what happened. The details of the image may be added and not represent the actual details present on the original occasion. The person experiencing the vivid image would have no way of knowing whether he was experiencing events as they happened or as a reconstruction of events.

The data provided by surgeons are claimed to support two theoretical stands. One is that everything experienced goes into the permanent memory system. The other is that whatever goes into the permanent memory system is there permanently. The second of these propositions has somewhat greater plausibility than the first. Nearly all experimental evidence suggests that only a very small fraction of the information that enters the short-term memory system is ever recorded in the long-term system. The extent to which the long-term memory system provides a permanent storage system is an issue related to the commonly asked question of whether anything learned is ever really forgotten.

One mechanism that may produce a forgetting effect is a failure of the retrieval system, a matter about which comments have already been made. Other forgetting may occur because of a failure in the retention mechanism itself. Within the latter mechanism, deterioration may be attributed to two general classes of phenomena. One is a decay of the memory trace, and the other is the interference that one trace may produce by the formation or action of another trace.

Let us first consider the decay theory of forgetting. This theory gains much support from personal experience but little from scientific experimentation. If information in long-term storage is held at the synapses, through chemical changes during learning, it may well be that the chemical process may be reversible and that time will slowly restore the chemical state that existed prior to learning. So far no one has been able to demonstrate either that decay occurs as a natural process or that no decay occurs. The majority of learning theorists have taken the position that learning represents an irreversible process, but that it is subject to disruption through learning at some other time. Decay theory is plausible in terms of one's own personal experience, which gives the impression that memories slowly fade, but experimentation shows that decay is not the major phenomenon involved. Here, as in other phases of the study of man's information system, theory derived from personal experience has been extremely misleading.

Although the decay theory of forgetting finds little experimental support, there is overwhelming evidence that one item of information learned can interfere with the learning or recall of other items of information. When the learning of an item of information interferes with the retention of an item of information subsequently learned, the interference thus produced is referred to as *proactive inhibition*. When an item of information learned interferes with the retention of an item of information previously learned, then the effect is called *retroactive inhibition*. Both effects are very pronounced in laboratory experiments and can be considered sufficient in size to account for much of forgetting. Everyday experience demonstrates these phenomena. When my secretary, Jenny Gallagher, marries and becomes Jenny Malloney, I may have difficulty in remembering her new name, because I am so firmly committed to thinking of her as Jenny Gallagher. Learning her original name interferes with both the learning and retention of her new name. But ultimately I master her new name, and then one day I try to recall her maiden name and cannot.

The learning of the new name has interfered with the recall of the old name. These are the phenomena of proactive inhibition and retroactive inhibition that are believed to account for most of what is called forgetting.

Although these phenomena have been given fancy names, little is known about what they really involve. For example, when I cannot recall the maiden name of Jenny Malloney, is it because the learning of the new name has eradicated the memory of the old name? The answer is "probably not," for what may have happened is that when I learned to refer to her as Jenny Malloney, I have also learned at the same time *not* to say Jenny Gallagher. In learning *not* to respond in a particular way, one is learning an inhibition. It may be that in learning to inhibit the response of saying Jenny Gallagher, I have learned the inhibition so well that I have become unable to make the response at all, even when I want to. The evidence is not sufficient to show whether interference works through producing inhibitions or through actually eradicating the record, though the inhibition theory is at present the more popular. The interference theory of forgetting seems to be basically sound, but at this time there is little known about how interference works.

Interference processes have been shown, in experimental situations, to produce phenomena closely similar to those ordinarily described as forgetting. Both short-term memory and long-term memory are subject to this effect. The information in short-term storage also appears to undergo a rather rapid decay through time. If one could find a situation in which information placed in long-term memory could be held without being interfered with by other learning, then one might be able to find out whether decay also takes place in the more permanent system of storage. There is one situation which permits one to do this. Material learned just before sleep should not be subject to interference during sleep when there is no learning taking place. A number of well-known experiments have been conducted in such a setting, and the results have shown very little decay during sleep of material learned just before sleep. Such evidence gives some support to the idea that most forgetting is produced by interference.

A Concluding Comment

This brief volume has provided only the most sketchy outline of one of the most rapidly developing areas of knowledge where psychology, physiology, and information theory come together to produce information-processing models of perception and learning. The author believes that such models are those that the media specialist and the educational technologist are most likely to find useful during the next few years and that these practitioners should become thoroughly acquainted with research related to them. This small book can only begin to whet the reader's appetite for such knowledge and cannot provide the full and strong foundation that the practitioners in the educational field are probably going to require.

References

Adams, J. A. *Human memory*. New York: McGraw-Hill, 1967.

Allen, J. E., & Travers, R. M. W. Retention as a function of rate of information transmission and degree of compression. *Florida Journal of Educational Research*, 1967, **9**, 3–9.

Averbach, E., & Coriell, A. S. Short-term memory in vision. *Bell System Technical Journal*, 1961, **40**, 309–328.

Bartlett, F. C. *Remembering*. Cambridge: Cambridge University Press, 1932.

Berlyne, D. E. *Conflict, arousal and curiosity*. New York: McGraw-Hill, 1960.

Bower, T. G. R. Visual selection: scanning vs. filtering. *Psychonomic Science*, 1965, **3**, 561–562.

Bower, T. G. R. The visual world of infants. *Scientific American*, 1966, **215**, 80–92.

Broadbent, D. E. *Perception and communication*. New York: Pergamon Press, 1958.

Broadbent, D. E. Attention and the perception of speech. *Scientific American*, 1962, **206**, 143–151.

Broadbent, D. E. Some recent research from the applied psychology research unit. In J. J. McGrath & D. E. Buckner (Eds.), *Vigilance*. New York: McGraw-Hill, 1963. Pp. 78–82.

Brown, L. T., & Farha, W. Some physical determinants of viewing time under three instructional sets. *Perception and Psychophysics*, 1966, **1**, 2–4.

Chapanis, A. *Man-machine engineering*. Belmont, Calif.: Wadsworth, 1965.

Cherry, E. C. Some experiments on the recognition of speech. *Journal of the Acoustical Society of America*, 1953, **25**, 975–979.

Cooper, J. C., & Gaeth, J. H. Interactions of modality with age and meaningfulness in verbal learning. *Journal of Educational Psychology*, 1967, **58**, 41–44.

Corcoran, D. W. J. Acoustic factors in proofreading. *Nature*, 1967, **214**, 851–852.

Day, W. F., & Beach, B. R. *A survey of the research literature comparing the visual and auditory presentation of information*. University of Virginia, Contract No. W33-039-ac-21269, E. O. No. 694–37, November 1950.

Dewey, J. *The sources of a science of education.* New York: Liveright, 1929.

Feigenbaum, E. A., & Simon, H. A. Brief notes on EPAM theory of verbal learning. In C. N. Cofer (Ed.), *Verbal behavior and learning.* New York: McGraw-Hill, 1963.

Fogel, L. J. *Human information processing.* Englewood, N.J.: Prentice-Hall, 1967.

Fowler, H. *Curiosity and exploratory behavior.* New York: Macmillan, 1965.

Gibson, J. *The perception of the visual world.* Boston: Houghton Mifflin, 1950.

Gibson, J. *The senses considered as perceptual systems.* Boston: Houghton Mifflin, 1966.

Gibson, E. J., & Yonas, A. A developmental study of visual search behavior. *Perception and Psychophysics,* 1966, **1,** 169–171.

Gregory, R. L. *Eye and brain.* New York: McGraw-Hill, 1966.

Hake, H. W., Rodwan, A., & Weintraub, D. Noise reduction in perception. In K. R. Hammond (Ed.), *The psychology of Egon Brunswick.* New York: Holt, Rinehart and Winston, 1966. Pp. 277–316.

Halle, M., & Stevens, K. Speech recognition: a model and a program for research. *IRE Transactions,* 1962, IT-8. 155–159.

Hartline, H. K., & Ratliff, F. Inhibitory interaction of receptor units in the eye of limulus. *Journal of General Physiology,* 1956–57, **40,** 357–376.

Head, H. *Studies in neurology.* Oxford: Oxford University Press, 1920.

Hebb, D. O. *The organization of behavior.* New York: Wiley, 1949.

Hebb, D. O. *Textbook of psychology.* (2nd ed.) Philadelphia: Saunders, 1966.

Hebb, D. O. Concerning imagery. *Psychological Review,* 1968, **75,** 466–477.

Henneman, R. H., & Long, E. R. *A comparison of the visual and auditory senses as channels for data presentation.* Wright Air Development Center Technical Report, 1954, 54–363, 41 pp. (mimeographed).

Hubel, D. H. The visual cortex of the brain. *Scientific American,* 1963, **209,** 54–62.

Hubel, D. H., & Wiesel, T. N. Receptive fields of single neurones in the cat's striate cortex. *Journal of Physiology,* 1959, **148,** 574–591.

Hull, C. L. *Essentials of behavior.* New Haven: Yale University Press, 1951.

Jacobson, H. The information capacity of the human eye. *Science,* 1951, **113,** 292–293. (a)

Jacobson, H. Information and the human ear. *Journal of the Acoustical Society of America,* 1951, **23,** 463–471. (b)

Jester, R. E., & Travers, R. M. W. Comprehension of connected meaningful discourse as a function of rate and mode of presentation. *Journal of Educational Research,* 1966, **59,** 297–302.

Judson, A. J., Cofer, C. N., & Gelfand, S. Reasoning as an associative process; II, "direction" in problem solving as a function of prior reinforcement of relevant responses. *Psychological Reports,* 1956, **2,** 501–507.

Knowlton, J. Q. On the definition of "picture." *Audiovisual Communications Review,* 1966, **14,** 157–183.

Lettvin, J. Y., Matturana, H. R., McCullough, W. S., & Pitts, W. H. What the frog's eye tells the frog's brain. *Proceedings of the Institute of Radio Engineers,* 1959, **47,** 1940–1951.

Liberman, A. M. Some results of research on speech perception. *Journal of the Acoustical Society of America,* 1957, **29,** 117–123.

Lovejoy, E. *Attention in discrimination learning.* San Francisco: Holden-Day, 1968.

Mackworth, N. H., & Morandi, A. J. The gaze selects informative details within pictures. *Perception and Psychophysics,* 1967, **2,** 547–551.

Miller, G. A. The magic number 7, plus or minus two: some limits on our capacity for processing information. *Psychological Review,* 1956, **63,** 81–97.

Miller, G. A., Galanter, E. H., & Pribram, K. H. *Plans and the structure of behavior.* New York: Holt, 1960.

Milner, P. M. The cell assembly: Mark II. *Psychological Review,* 1957. **64,** 242–252.

Mueller, D. J., & Travers, R. M. W. Temporal relations and meaningfulness in paired-associate learning. *Psychological Reports,* 1965, **17,** 491–497.

Muntz, W. R. A. Mechanics of visual form recognition in animals. In Weiant Walthen-Dunn (Ed.), *Models for the perception of speech and visual form.* Cambridge: M.I.T. Press, 1964. Pp. 126–136.

National Physical Laboratory, Symposium No. 10. *The mechanization of thought processes.* London: Her Majesty's Stationery Office, 1959.

Neisser, U. Visual search. *Scientific American,* 1964, **210,** 94–102.

Neisser, U. *Cognitive psychology.* New York: Appleton-Century-Crofts, 1967.

Nuttin, J., & Greenwald, A. G. *Reward and punishment in human learning.* New York: Academic Press, 1968.

Overing, R. L. R., & Travers, R. M. W. Effect upon transfer of variations in training conditions. *Journal of Educational Psychology,* 1966, **57,** 179–188.

Overing, R. L. R., & Travers, R. M. W. Variation in the amount of irrelevant cues in training and test conditions and the effect upon transfer. *Journal of Educational Psychology,* 1967, **58,** 62–68.

Pierce, J. R., & Karlin, J. E. Reading rates and the information rate of the human channels. *Bell System Technical Journal,* 1957, **36,** 497–516.

Pollack, I. The information of elementary auditory displays, II. *Journal of the Acoustical Society of America,* 1953, **25,** 765–769.

Pollack, I., & Ficks, L. Information of elementary multidimensional displays. *Journal of the Acoustical Society of America,* 1954, **26,** 155–158.

Quastler, H., & Wulff, V. J. *Human performance in information transmission.* Control Systems Laboratory Report No. 62, University of Illinois, 1955.

Rabbitt, P. M. A. Ignoring irrelevant information. *British Journal of Psychology,* 1964, **55,** 403–414.

Rappaport, M. The role of redundancy in the discrimination of visual forms. *Journal of Experimental Psychology,* 1957, **53,** 3–10.

Reid, I., & Travers, R. M. W. Time required to switch attention. *American Educational Research Journal,* 1968, **5,** 203–211.

Selfridge, O. G. Pandemonium: a paradigm for learning. In National Physical Laboratory, Symposium No. 10, *The mechanization of thought processes.* London: Her Majesty's Stationery Office, 1959. Pp. 513–531.

Shannon, C. E. A mathematical theory of communication. *Bell System Technical Journal,* 1949, **27,** 379–423 and 623–656.

Solley, C. M., & Murphy, G. *Development of the perceptual world.* New York: Basic Books, 1960.

Sperling, G. On the information available in brief visual presentations. *Psychological Monographs,* 1960, **74,** No. 11.

Strongman, K. T., & Brown, R. Visual search with meaningful and non-meaningful material. *Quarterly Journal of Experimental Psychology,* 1966, **18,** 164–168.

Sutherland, N. S. Stimulus analyzing mechanisms. In National Physical Laboratory, Symposium No. 10, *The mechanization of thought processes.* London: Her Majesty's Stationery Office, 1959. Pp. 575–601.

Thomas, H. Visual-fixation responses of infants to stimuli of varying complexity. *Child Development,* 1965, **36,** 629–638.

Travers, R. M. W., *Research and theory related to audiovisual information transmission.* (Rev. ed.) U.S. Department of Health, Education, and Welfare, Office of Education Contract No. 3-20-003, 1967.

Travers, R. M. W. *A study of the advantages and disadvantages of using simplified visual presentations in instructional materials.* Final Report on Grant No. OEG-1-7-070144-5235, U.S. Office of Education, 1969.

Travers, R. M. W., & Chan, A. The effect on retention of labeling visual displays. *American Educational Research Journal,* 1966, **3,** 55–67.

Travers, R. M. W., Chan, A., & Van Mondfrans, A. P. The effect of colored embellishment of a visual array on a simultaneously presented audio array. *Audiovisual Communications Review,* 1965, **13,** 159–164.

Travers, R. M. W., & Mueller, D. J. Temporal relations and meaningfulness in paired-associate learning. *Psychological Reports,* 1965, **17,** 491–497.

Triesman, A. M. Contextual cues in selective listening. *Quarterly Journal of Experimental Psychology,* 1960, **12,** 242–248.

Van Mondfrans, A. P., & Travers, R. M. W. Paired-associate learning within and across sense modalities and involving simultaneous and sequential presentations. *American Educational Research Journal,* 1965, **2,** 89–99.

Vickery, B. C. *On retrieval system theory.* London: Butterworths, 1965.

Vitz, P. C. Preference for different amounts of visual complexity. *Behavioral Science,* 1966, **11,** 105–114.

Von Senden, M. *Space and sight.* (Translated by Peter Heath). Glencoe, Ill.: Free Press, 1960. (Orig. pub. in German, 1932.)

Walk, R. D., & Gibson, E. J. A comparative and analytic study of visual depth perception. *Psychological Monographs,* 1961, **75,** No. 15.

Warren, R. M. Verbal transformation effect and auditory perceptual mechanisms. *Psychological Bulletin,* 1968, **70,** 261–270.

Wickelgren, W. A. Acoustic similarity and retroactive interference in short-term memory. *Journal of Verbal Learning and Verbal Behavior,* 1965, **4,** 53–62. (a)

Wickelgren, W. A. Short-term memory for phonemically similar lists. *American Journal of Psychology,* 1965, **78,** 567–574. (b)

Wickelgren, W. A. Phonemic similarity and interference in short-term memory for single letters. *Journal of Experimental Psychology,* 1966, **71,** 396–404.

Index